The Caucasian Chalk Circle

BERTOLT BRECHT

# The Caucasian Chalk Circle

English Version by Eric Bentley

University of Minnesota Press
Minneapolis

Published by the University of Minnesota Press
111 Third Avenue South, Suite 290
Minneapolis, MN 55401-2520
http://www.upress.umn.edu

Library of Congress Cataloging-in-Publication Data

Brecht, Bertolt, 1898–1956.
    [Kaukasische Kreidekreis. English]
    The caucasian chalk circle / Bertolt Brecht ; English version by
Eric Bentley.
      p.    cm.
    Originally published in *Parables for the Theatre: Two Plays by
Bertolt Brecht* (Minneapolis: University of Minnesota Press, 1948).
    Includes bibliographical references.
    ISBN 978-0-8166-3528-3 (pbk. : alk. paper)
    I. Bentley, Eric, 1916–    II. Title.
    PT2603.R397.K3913    1999
    832'.912                           99-046426

Printed in the United States of America on acid-free paper

The University of Minnesota is an equal-opportunity educator and employer.

22 21 20 19 18 17 16            10 9 8 7

# Contents

# Preface

*Eric Bentley*

Bertolt Brecht wrote *The Caucasian Chalk Circle* in California as World War II was drawing to a close. He thought of it (sometimes, at least) as a contribution to the American musical theater, and it had its world premiere in the United States in 1948 at Carleton College in Minnesota. The director was one of my graduate students at the University of Minnesota, and I myself directed the first professional production of the play, which took place later that year at the Hedgerow Theatre in Pennsylvania.

It was in that year too that the University of Minnesota Press published *Parables for the Theatre*, a volume that comprised both *Chalk Circle* and *The Good Woman of Setzuan*. That book proved to be Brecht's best seller down the years, and is still in print under the same title in British territory (a Penguin paperback). In the United States, after a while, the two plays were separately published, and they are so published again, now, in 1999.

The translation of *Chalk Circle* was revised for the production at Lincoln Center, New York, in 1966, but, unlike *The Good Woman*, it was never really "adapted" or abridged. Whereas the text of *Good Woman* seemed to beg for abridgment, the text of

*Chalk Circle* seemed to ask for the respectful handling of every speech, every line, almost every word. One exception to this rule, however, requires a degree of explanation.

This exception was a Prologue that actually had not been part of Brecht's original plan for the play, but was prompted by events in Russia at the time — by, in fact, the Russian victory over the armies of Hitler. Brecht decided to frame his play with a scene in which Russian land reclaimed by the Germans is to be assigned to whomever the Russians decide to assign it to. Brecht advised me not to include the Prologue in the first printing of the *Parables,* and indeed it was not to be included for another eleven years. The Prologue was first performed in Minneapolis when the Minnesota Theater Company staged *Chalk Circle* in 1965.

When the play was performed in Harvard's then new Loeb Drama Center in 1960, Brecht's Prologue had been prefaced by these words of mine:

> Friends old and new, we ask tonight
> Who owns a child and by what right?
> There is a bit of Chinese lore
> About a circle chalked upon the floor...
> Two different women claim one child
> Their quarrel drives the neighbors wild
> So they betake them to the king
> Who with some chalk describes a ring
> Around the infant where he stands.
> "Take him," the king says, "by the hands
> And pull! She who can get him out
> Must be his mother without a doubt."
> One woman briskly goes to work
> And pulls the child out with a jerk.
> The other doesn't have the heart
> For fear she'll tear the child apart.
> "Which," quoth the king, "proves that this other

Who would not harm him is his mother."
The logic's bad. Only the blind
Could hold that mothers all are kind.
And yet one hopes the king's surmise
Chanced to be right for otherwise
What a disturbing situation:
The mother an abomination
While the false claimant is a love —
A crisis that won't bear thinking of
Like: who owns Natchez or Birmingham?
Santo Domingo? Or Vietnam?
The crisis spared the Chinese king
We now shall face — this evening —
And tell a touched-up tale in which
The actual mother is a bitch.
Even the circle chalked on the floor
Will not be what it was before.

When in 1966 the play was slated to have a Broadway-scale production at Lincoln Center, there were lengthy discussions of the Prologue, pro and con. The pros carried the day, but I was asked to do an abridgment of it. As something of a Brecht loyalist at the time, I opposed this plan. Yet the result pleased me, and eventually (in 1983) I used the shortened version in print. It is used again here.

# Comments on
## *The Caucasian Chalk Circle*
## from *Bentley on Brecht*

### *Eric Bentley*

The text of this section consists of an essay written at the time of the Lincoln Center production of *The Caucasian Chalk Circle* (1966) and then variously published until its eventual inclusion in *Bentley on Brecht*.

In the prologue to *The Caucasian Chalk Circle,* the people of two collective farms in Georgia debate their respective titles to the ownership of a piece of land. Up to now it has belonged to one farm, but now the other claims to be able to make better use of it. Who should own *anything?* Should possession be nine-tenths of the law? Or should law and possession be open to review? That is the question Brecht raises. In the first draft of the play, the date of this bit of action was the 1930s. Later, Brecht shifted it to 1945 for two reasons: so that the land can be approached as a new problem, in that the farmers on it had all been ordered east at the approach of Hitler's armies; and so that the farmers newly claiming it can have partially earned it by having fought as partisans against the invader.

The prologue is a bit of a shock for American audiences. Here are all these communists — Russians at that — calling each other Comrades, and so on. That is why, until recently, the prologue was always omitted from American productions. In 1965, however, it was included in the Minnesota Theater Company's production without untoward incidents or, so far as I know, outraged comment. With the years the prologue had not changed, but the world had. America had. The existence of the U.S.S.R. is now conceded in the U.S.A. That communists do use the title "Comrades" is taken in stride. There is even understanding for the fact that the playwright Bertolt Brecht sympathized with communism in those days, more consistently than Jean-Paul Sartre and Peter Weiss do today.

However, disapproval of the prologue is not caused merely by the labels. A deeper malaise is caused by the *mode* of the dispute over the land. Land has always been fought over, often with guns. The expectation that some individual should pull a gun, or threaten to, is part of our stock response to the situation, but in the prologue, this expectation receives a calculated disappointment. The conflict is, or has been, real, but a new way of resolving it has been found, a new attitude to antagonists has been found. Not to mention the new solution: the land goes to the interlopers, the impostors, because they offer convincing evidence that they will be able to make better use of it. Both the conclusion and the road by which it is reached imply a reversal of the values by which our civilization has been living.

And Soviet civilization? Were we to visit Georgia, should we witness such decisions being made, and being arrived at in Brecht's way? It is open to doubt, even in 1966, while, in 1945, nothing could have been more misleading than Brecht's prologue, if it was intended to give an accurate picture of Stalin's Russia. We hear that Soviet citizens have themselves complained that, quite apart from the political point, they find nothing recognizably Russian in this German scene.

Is it thereby invalidated? "The home of the Soviet people shall also be the home of Reason!" That is certainly a key line in the prologue, but the verb is "shall be," not "is." That Brecht aligned himself with socialism, and saw the Soviet Union as the chief champion of socialism, is clear, yet is only to say that he saw Russia as on the right path, not by any means as having arrived at the goal. Let the worried reader of the prologue to *The Caucasian Chalk Circle* also read Brecht's poem "Are the People Infallible?" in which the poet speaks in this vein of the death in 1939 of the Soviet playwright Tretyakov:

*1*

*My teacher*
*Who was great, who was kind*
*Has been shot, sentenced by a People's Court.*
*As a spy. His name has been condemned.*
*His books have been annihilated. Conversation about him*
*Is suspect and has subsided.*
*Suppose he is innocent?*

*2*

*The sons of the people have found him guilty.*
*The collective farms and factories of the workers*
*The most heroic institutions in the world*
*Have found in him an enemy.*
*No voice was raised on his behalf.*
*Suppose he is innocent?*

*3*

*The people have many enemies.*
*In the highest positions*
*Sit enemies. In the most useful laboratories*
*Sit enemies. They build*
*Canals and dams for the good of whole continents and the canals*
*Clog up and the dams*
*Collapse. The man in charge must be shot.*
*Suppose he is innocent?*

### 4

*The enemy walks in disguise.*
*He draws a worker's cap down over his face. His friends*
*Know him for a zealous worker. His wife*
*Displays the holes in his shoes:*
*He went through his shoes in the service of the people.*
*And yet he is an enemy. Was my teacher such a man?*
*Suppose he is innocent?*

### 5

*To speak about the enemies who may be sitting in the courts of*
  *the people*
*Is dangerous. For the courts have to be respected.*
*To demand papers with the proofs of guilt on them in black and*
  *white*
*Is senseless. For there need not be any such papers.*
*Criminals hold proofs of their innocence in their hands.*
*The innocent often have no proofs.*
*Is it best, then, to be silent?*
*Suppose he is innocent?*

### 6

*What 5000 have built, one man can destroy.*
*Among 50 who are sentenced*
*One may be innocent.*
*Suppose he is innocent?*

### 7

*On the supposition that he is innocent*
*What will he be thinking as he goes to his death?*

In any case, to prove Brecht wrong about Russia would not necessarily be to prove him wrong about socialism.

A socialist play, is this play for socialists only? That is for non-socialists to decide. From Brecht's viewpoint, a lot of people are potential socialists who might — at this time, in this place — be surprised to hear it. It is a play for all who are not identified with those it shows to be the common enemy, and it may turn out to be a play even for some of those who are identified with the enemy, since they may not recognize the identification, preferring a life-illusion. French aristocrats applauded *Figaro. The Threepenny Opera* must have been enjoyed by many who, very shortly afterward, voted for Hitler.

The prologue shows a country (forget it is Russia, if that offends you) where Reason has made inroads upon Unreason. Unreason, in *The Caucasian Chalk Circle,* takes the form of private property, and the laws that guarantee it. "Property is theft," and, by paradox, a private person who steals another private person's property, infringing the law, only reenacts the original rape of the earth, and confirms the law — of private property. The characters in *Chalk Circle* who most firmly believe in private property are most actively engaged in fighting over private property — whether to cling to it or to grab it.

Where is private property's most sensitive spot? One learns the answer when a businessman announces that his son will be taking over the business or when a spokesman for all things holy comes to his favorite theme of mother and child.

> . . . of all ties, the ties of blood are strongest. Mother and child, is there a more intimate relationship? Can one tear a child from its mother? High Court of Justice, she has conceived it in the holy ecstasies of love, she has carried it in her womb, she has fed it with her blood, she has borne it with pain. . . .

This is the voice of one of the spokesmen for all things holy in *The Caucasian Chalk Circle,* and so, when the possession of a child has been in dispute, whether at the court of Solomon in Israel, or before a Chinese magistrate in the year A.D. 1000, the question asked has been only: Which womb did it come out of? Which loins begat it? The ultimate *locus* of private property is in the private parts.

Plato had other plans. He knew that a given parent may be the worst person to bring up his or her child. Our concern, he assumes, should be to produce the best human beings, the best society, not to sacrifice these ends to an, after all, arbitrary notion of "natural" right. The point about an umbilical cord is that it has to be cut. Children should be assigned to those best qualified to bring them up. . . . Plato's Republic *is* "the home of Reason."

The Georgia of *The Caucasian Chalk Circle* is not. After a prologue which provides a hint of what it would mean to begin to create a home for Reason on this earth, the play transports us to a world which, for all its exotic externals, is nothing other than the world we live in, *our* world, the world of Unreason, of Disorder, of Injustice. Those who are upset by the idealizations of the prologue, by its "utopianism," need not fret. The play itself provides an image of life in its customary mode — soiled, stinking, cruel, outrageous.

Even in a jungle, lovely flowers will spring up here and there, such being the fecundity of nature, and however badly our pastors and masters run our society, however much they pull to pieces that which they claim to be keeping intact, nature remains fecund, human beings are born with human traits, sometimes human strength outweighs human weakness, and human grace shows itself amid human ugliness. "In the bloodiest times," as our play has it, "there are kind people." Their kindness is arbitrary. No sociologist could deduce it from the historical process. Just the contrary. It represents the brute refusal of nature to be submerged in history and therefore, arguably (and this *is* Brecht's argument), the possibility that the creature should, at some future point, subdue history.

For the present, though — a present that has spread itself out through the whole course of historical time — the sociologists win, and man is not the master but the slave of society. History is the history of power struggles conducted (behind the moralistic rhetoric familiar to us all from the mass media) with minimum scrupulousness and maximum violence. To give way to the promptings of nature, to natural sympathy, to the natural love of the Good, is to be a Sucker. America invented that expressive word, and America's most articulate comedian, W. C. Fields, called one of his films *Never Give a Sucker an Even Break*. Which is the credo of Western civilization as depicted in the works of Bertolt Brecht.

In *The Caucasian Chalk Circle* a sucker gets an even break. That seems contradictory, and in the contradiction lies the whole interest of the story. Or rather of its second part. In the first part, we see the inevitable working itself out. The sucker — the good girl who gives way to her goodness — is not given any breaks at all. She is punished for her non-sin, her anti-sin. She loses everything, both the child she has saved and adopted, and the soldier-fiancé whom she has loyally loved and waited for. She is abandoned, isolated, stripped, torn apart, like other people in Brecht's plays and our world who persist in the practice of active goodness.

> The Ironshirts took the child, the beloved child.
> The unhappy girl followed them to the city, the dreaded city.
> She who had borne him demanded the child.
> She who had raised him faced trial.

So ends Part I: a complete Brecht play in itself. In Part II Brecht was determined to put the question: Suppose the inevitable did not continue to work itself out? Now how could he do this? By having a socialist revolution destroy private property and establish the rule of Reason? That is what he would have done, had he been as narrow and doctrinaire as some readers of his prologue assume. But what is in the prologue is not in the play itself. For the second half of his play Brecht invented a new version of the Chalk Circle legend, which is also a new version of another idea from literary tradition, the idea that the powers that be can sometimes be temporarily overthrown and a brief Golden Age ensue.

Who will decide the case?
To whom will the child be assigned?
Who will the judge be? A good judge? A bad?
The city was in flames.
In the judge's seat sat — Azdak.

Inevitably, necessarily, a judge in the society depicted in *The Caucasian Chalk Circle* must assign a child to its actual mother. In that proposition, the law of private property seems to receive the sanction of Mother Nature herself — that is to say, the owners of private property are able to appeal to nature without conscious irony. Such an event, however, would give Brecht at best a brief epilogue to Part I. What gives him a second part to his play, and one which enables him in the end to pick up the loose ends left by the prologue, is that the judge is Azdak, and that Azdak is a mock king, an Abbot of Unreason, a Lord of Misrule, who introduces "a brief Golden Age, almost an age of justice." As F. M. Cornford writes in *The Origin of Attic Comedy,*

The reign of Zeus stood in the Greek mind for the existing moral and social order; its overthrow, which is the theme of so many of the comedies, might be taken to symbolize . . . the breaking up of all ordinary restraints, or again . . . the restoration of the Golden Age of Justice and Lovingkindness, that Age of Kronos which lingered in the imagination of poets, like the afterglow of a sun that had set below the horizon of the Age of Iron. The seasonal festivals of a Saturnalian character celebrated the return, for a brief interregnum, of a primitive innocence that knew not shame, and a liberty that at any other time would have been licentious. Social ranks were inverted, the slave exercising authority over the master. At Rome each household became a miniature republic, the slaves being invested with the dignities of office. A mock king was chosen to bear rule during the festival, like the medieval Abbot of Unreason or Lord of Misrule.

In this case, how is the play any different from the prologue, except in the temporariness of Azdak's project? Its temporariness is of a piece with its precariousness, its freakishness, its skittishness, its semiaccidental character. Only with a touch of irony can one say that Azdak establishes a Golden Age or even that he is a good judge. The age remains far from golden, and his judging is often outrageous enough. But his *extra*ordinary outrages call our attention to the ordinary outrages of ordinary times — to the fact that outrage *is* ordinary, is the usual thing, and that we are shocked, not by injustice per se, but only by injustice that favors the poor and the weak. Azdak did not rebuild a society, nor even start a movement that had such an end in view. He only provided Georgia with something to think about and us with a legend, a memory, an image.

So much for the ideological *schema*. The play would be too rigidly schematic if Brecht had just brought together the Good Girl with the Appropriate Judge, using both characters simply as mouthpieces for a position. But there is more to both of them than that.

Discussing the role of the Ironical Man in ancient comedy, F. M. Cornford remarks that "the special kind of irony" he practices is

> feigned stupidity. The word Ironist itself in the fifth century appears to mean "cunning" or (more exactly) "sly." Especially it meant the man who masks his batteries of deceit behind a show of ordinary good nature or indulges a secret pride and conceit of wisdom, while he affects ignorance and self-depreciation, but lets you see all the while that he could enlighten you if he chose, and so makes a mock of you. It was for putting on these airs that Socrates was accused of "irony" by his enemies.

This passage sets forth what I take to be the preliminary design of Azdak's character, but then Brecht complicates the design. Azdak is not simply an embodiment of an ironical viewpoint, he is a person with a particular history, who needs irony for a particular reason—and not all the time. It is through the chinks in the ironical armor that we descry the man. *Azdak is not being ironical when he tells us he wanted to denounce himself for letting the Grand Duke escape.* He supposed that, while the Grand Duke and his Governors were busy fighting the Princes, the carpet weavers had brought off a popular revolution, and, as a revolutionary, he wished to denounce himself for a counter-revolutionary act.

What kind of revolutionary was he? A very modern kind: a disenchanted one. Those who like to compare Azdak the judge to Robin Hood should not fail to compare Azdak the politician to Arthur Koestler. Before the present revolt of the carpet weavers, decades earlier, there had been another popular uprising. Azdak maintains, or pretends, that this was in his grandfather's time, forty years ago, and not in Georgia, but in Persia. His two songs—which lie at the very heart of our play—tell both of the conditions that produced the uprising and of the uprising itself.[1] The pretense is that revolution represents disorder, and the suppression of revolutions, order; and that Azdak is appealing to the Generals to restore order. This last item is not a hollow pretense or a single irony, for Azdak has not championed revolt. He has withdrawn into his shell. His job as a "village scrivener" is the outward token of the fact. In a note, Brecht advises the actor of the role not to imagine that Azdak's rags directly indicate his character. He wears them, Brecht says, as a Shakespearean clown wears the motley of a fool. Azdak is not lacking in wisdom. Only it is the bitter wisdom of the disillusioned intellectual, and, in Brecht's view, a partly false wisdom prompted not alone by objective facts but quite as much by the "wise" man's own limitations.

Azdak has the characteristic limitation of the Brechtian rogue: cowardice. Or at any rate: courage insufficient to the occasion. He is Brecht's Herr Keuner saying no to tyranny only after the tyrant is safely dead. At least, this is how Azdak is, if left to himself. Yet, like other human beings, he is not a fixed quantity but influenceable by the flow of things, and especially by the people he meets. A passive sort of fellow, he acts less than he *re*acts. Our play describes his reaction to a new and unforeseen situation, and especially, in the end, to a single person: Grusha. Which gives the last section of the play its organic movement.

Azdak needs drawing out, and what Brecht does is expose him to a series of persons and situations that do draw him out. (That he also brings with him into the Golden Age his unregenerate self creates the comic contradictions. It is hard, through all the little trial scenes, to tell where selfishness leaves off and generosity begins: this is a source of amusement, and also enables Brecht to question accepted assumptions on the relation of social and antisocial impulses.) The Test of the Chalk Circle with which the action culminates does not follow automatically from the philosophy of Azdak but is a product of a dramatic development. At the outset he is in no mood to be so good or so wise. He has just been mercilessly beaten, but then he reacts in his especially sensitive way to all that ensues, and above all to the big speech in which Grusha denounces him:

AZDAK: Fined twenty piasters!

GRUSHA: Even if it was thirty, I'd tell you what I think of your justice, you drunken onion! How dare you talk to me like the cracked Isaiah on the church window? As if you were somebody. You weren't born to this. You weren't born to rap your own mother on the knuckles if she swipes a little bowl of salt someplace. Aren't you ashamed when you see how I tremble before you? You've made yourself their servant so they won't get their houses stolen out from under them—houses they themselves stole! Since when did a house belong to its bedbugs? But you're their watchdog, or how would they get our men into their wars? Bribe taker! I don't respect you. No more than a thief or a bandit with a knife. Do what you like. You can all do what you like, a hundred against one, but do you know who should be chosen for a profession like yours? Extortioners! Men who rape children! Let it be their punishment to sit in judgment on their fellowmen! Which is worse than to hang from the gallows.

AZDAK: Now it is thirty.

She could hardly know how she got under his skin. Her denunciation, quite guileless and spontaneous, happens to be couched in just the terms that come home to him. For she is representing him as a traitor to his class. Who does he think he is, who is now setting himself up as a Lord over his own people? Well, in his own view, Azdak *was* something of a traitor to his class, but he has been busy for a year or two trying to make it up to them, and now Grusha is providing him with the happiest of all occasions to prove this. His decision to give her the child grows out of his sense of guilt and out of his delight in opportunities to make good.

One could say, too, that his earlier confrontation with Granny Grusinia prepares the way for the later one with Grusha. Here, too, he has to be drawn out, partly by threats, but even more by finding again his original identification with the cause of the people. Between them, Granny Grusinia and Grusha are the Marxian, Brechtian version of the "eternal feminine" whom our blundering, uncourageous Faust needs, if he is to move "onward and upward." Hence, although the Chalk Circle incident occupies only a minute or two at the end of a long play, it is rightly used for the title of the whole.

The incident not only clarifies the meaning of Azdak, it also brings together the various thematic threads of the play. In the first instance, there is the stated conclusion:

Take note what men of old concluded:
That what there is shall go to those who are good for it, thus:

Children to the motherly, that they prosper,
Carts to good drivers, that they be driven well,
The valley to the waterers, that it yield fruit.

But this was never in doubt. Any spectator who has spent the evening hoping for a surprise at the end courted disappointment. He should have been warned by the prologue. In an early draft Brecht planned to let the decision on the collective farms wait till the Chalk Circle story has been told. That, however, is politically ludicrous, if it means, as it would have to, that Soviet planners depend on folksingers in the way that some other leaders depend upon astrologers. And an infringement of a main principle of Brechtian drama would have occurred. In this type of play there should be no doubt as to what is going to happen, only as to how and why.

The valley is assigned to the waterers already in the prologue, and already in the first scenes that follow we see that Michael has had a bad mother but has been befriended by a better one. What remains to be said? On what grounds can we be asked to stay another couple of hours in the theater? One sufficient reason would be: to see Grusha *become* the mother. This is not Plato's Republic, and Grusha is no trained educator in a Platonic crèche. In the first phase of the action her purpose is only to rescue the child, not keep it: she is going to leave it on a peasant's doorstep and return home. We see the child becoming hers by stages, so that when Azdak reaches his verdict in the final scene, he is not having a brainstorm ("Grusha would be a splendid mother for this child") but recognizing an accomplished fact ("She *is* the mother of this child"). Another paradox: in this play that says possession is not nine-tenths of the law we learn that (in another sense) possession is ten-tenths of the law.

In the end, the child becomes Simon Shashava's too:

GRUSHA: You like him?

SIMON: With my respects, I like him.

GRUSHA: Now I can tell you: I took him because on that Easter Sunday I got engaged to you. So he's a child of love.

Michael had been a child of the lovelessness of his actual mother and the lifelessness of his actual father, but now it turns out that he will have a father who has been spared death in war and is very much alive, and a mother who did not love him at his conception, nor yet at his delivery, but who loves him *now*. The term "love child" is applied to bastards, and Michael, who was legitimate in the legal sense, however illegitimate humanly and morally, will now become a bastard in a sense which the story... legitimizes.

> Your father is a bandit
> A harlot the mother who bore you
> Yet honorable men
> Shall kneel down before you.
>
> Food to the baby horses
> The tiger's son will take.
> The mothers will get milk
> From the son of the snake.

Brecht's play broadens out into myth, and we hear many echoes — from the Bible, from Pirandello — but it is more relevant to see the phenomenon the other way around: not that Brecht lets his story spread outward toward other stories, but that he uses other stories, and mythical patterns, and pulls them in, brings them, as we say, "down to earth," in concrete, modern meanings. Most important, in this regard, is Brecht's use of what a Shakespearean scholar has called festive comedy. *The Caucasian Chalk Circle* is not an *inquiry* into the dispute over ownership presented in the prologue but a *celebration* of the assignment of the land to "those who are good for it."

A main preoccupation of this oldest form of comedy in Western tradition was with Impostors. *The Caucasian Chalk Circle* does this, for what could be a more gross imposture than the claims to either rulership or parenthood of the Abashwili couple? But Brecht does not leave the ancient patterns alone. Even as he turns around the old tale of the Chalk Circle, so also he plays his ironic, dialectical game with the patterns. *For Azdak and Grusha are impostors too.* That is what makes them brother and sister under the skin. In the impostor-mother, the impostor-judge recognizes his own.

> As if it was stolen goods she picked it up.
> As if she was a thief she sneaked away.

Thus the Singer, describing how Grusha got the baby. He is too generous. Legally, she *is* a thief; the child *is* stolen goods; and Azdak has "stolen" the judgeship, though, characteristically, not on his own initiative: he is a receiver of stolen goods. The special pleasure for Azdak in his Chalk Circle verdict is that, at the moment when he will return his own "stolen" goods to their "rightful" owners, he is able to give Grusha and Simon "their" child in (what they can hope is) perpetuity.

I have called the irony a game, for art is a game, but this is not to say that Brecht's playfulness is capricious. In the inversion lies the meaning, and it is simply our good fortune that there is fun in such things, that, potentially at least, there is fun in *all* human contradictions and oppositions. The old patterns have, indeed, no meaning for Brecht *until* they are inverted. For instance, this important pattern: the return to the Age of Gold. We, the modern audience, Russian or American, *return* to the Age of Gold when we see Azdak inverting our rules and laws. Azdak *returns* to an Age of Gold when he nostalgically recalls the popular revolt of a former generation. On the other hand, the Age of Azdak is not, literally, an Age of Gold at all. It is an age of war and internecine strife in which just a little justice can, by a fluke, be done. Nor is the traditional image of a Golden Age anything like a revolutionary's happy memories of days on the barricades: just the reverse. Finally, Brecht repudiates our hankering after past Ages of Gold altogether. That revolutions, for Azdak, are identified with the past is precisely what is wrong with him. In *The Caucasian Chalk Circle* we move back in order to move forward. The era of Azdak has the transitory character of the Saturnalia and so is properly identified with it. After the interregnum is over, the mock king goes back into anonymity, like Azdak. But the prologue suggests a *regnum* that is not accidental and short-lived but deliberate and perhaps not *inter*. And then there is the ultimate inversion: that the Golden Age should be envisaged not in the past but in the future, and not in fairyland or heaven, but in Georgia.

The Russian Georgia. But the American Georgia is included, at least in the sense that the play is about our twentieth-century world, and in a specific way. As Brecht saw things, this century came in on a wave of democratic hope. A new age was dawning, or seemed to be. So universally was this felt that the most powerful of counterrevolutionary movements, the Hitler movement, had to represent itself as socialist and announce, in its turn, the dawn of a new age. It could bring in no dawn of its own, of course, but in Germany it certainly prevented the arrival of the dawn that had seemed imminent.

This grouping of forces is what we have in *The Caucasian Chalk Circle*. A true dawn is promised by the rebellious carpet weavers. It never arrives, because the Ironshirts are paid to cut the weavers to pieces. At this point, when a triumphant Fat Prince enters, very much in the likeness of Marshal Goering, Azdak points at him with the comment: There's your new age all right! The thought of the new age, the longing for a new age, hovers over *The Caucasian Chalk Circle* from beginning to end, and any good production should seem haunted by it.

The prologue will say different things to different people as to what has already been achieved and where, but to all it conveys Brecht's belief that the new age is possible. What his audience is to be haunted by is not a memory, a fantasy, or a dream, but a possibility.

NOTES

1. Azdak's "Song of Chaos" is adapted from a translation of an ancient Egyptian lament, brought to notice in 1903, but dating back to about 2500 B.C. The document describes a state of social disintegration and revolt, appeals to the King and other authorities to take action. Brecht reverses the point of view, as his custom is, but since he does so ironically, he is able to stay close to such words of the original as the following:

Nay, but the highborn are full of lamentations, and the poor are full of joy. Every town saith: "Let us drive out the powerful from our midst."

Nay, but the son of the highborn man is no longer to be recognized. The child of his lady is become [no more than] the son of his handmaid.

Nay, but the boxes of ebony are broken up. Precious sesnem [sic] wood is cut in pieces for beds.

Nay, but the public offices are opened and their lists [of serfs] are taken away. Serfs become lords of serfs.

Behold, ladies lie on cushions [in lieu of beds] and magistrates in the storehouse. He that could not sleep upon walls now possesseth a bed.

Behold, he that never built for himself a boat now possesseth ships. He that possessed the same looketh at them, but they are no longer his.

(Translated from the Egyptian by A. M. Blackman, and published in *The Literature of the Ancient Egyptians* by Adolf Erman. London, 1927.)

# The Caucasian Chalk Circle

# Characters

OLD MAN *on the right*

PEASANT WOMAN *on the right*

YOUNG PEASANT

A VERY YOUNG WORKER

OLD MAN *on the left*

PEASANT WOMAN *on the left*

AGRICULTURIST KATO

GIRL TRACTORIST

WOUNDED SOLDIER

THE DELEGATE *from the capital*

THE SINGER

GEORGI ABASHWILI, *the Governor*

NATELLA, *the Governor's wife*

MICHAEL, *their son*

SHALVA, *an adjutant*

ARSEN KAZBEKI, *a fat prince*

MESSENGER *from the capital*

NIKO MIKADZE *and* MIKA LOLADZE, *doctors*

SIMON SHASHAVA, *a soldier*

GRUSHA VASHADZE, *a kitchen maid*

OLD PEASANT *with the milk*

CORPORAL *and* PRIVATE

PEASANT *and his wife*

LAVRENTI VASHNADZE, *Grusha's brother*

ANIKO, *his wife*

PEASANT WOMAN, *for a while Grusha's mother-in-law*

JUSSUP, *her son*

MONK

AZDAK, *village recorder*

SHAUWA, *a policeman*

GRAND DUKE

DOCTOR

INVALID

LIMPING MAN

BLACKMAILER

LUDOVICA

INNKEEPER, *her father-in-law*

STABLEBOY

POOR OLD PEASANT WOMAN

IRAKLI, *her brother-in-law, a bandit*

THREE WEALTHY FARMERS

ILLO SHUBOLADZE *and* SANDRO OBOLADZE, *lawyers*

OLD MARRIED COUPLE

SOLDIERS, SERVANTS, PEASANTS, BEGGARS,
MUSICIANS, MERCHANTS, NOBLES, ARCHITECTS

# Prologue

Summer of 1945.

*Among the ruins of a war-ravaged Caucasian village the* MEM-
BERS *of two Collective Farms, mostly women and older men, are
sitting in a circle, smoking and drinking wine. With them is a*
DELEGATE *of the State Reconstruction Commission from Tiflis,
the capital.*

PEASANT WOMAN, *left (pointing):* That's where we stopped
three Nazi tanks. But the apple orchard was already destroyed.
OLD MAN, *right:* Our beautiful dairy farm: a ruin.
GIRL TRACTORIST: I started the fire myself, Comrade. *(Pause.)*
DELEGATE: Comrades! Listen to the report. The Collective
Goat Farm Rosa Luxemburg, formerly located right here in
this valley, moved East, on orders from the government, at
the approach of Hitler's Armies. Now their plan is to return.
*(Delegates on right nod.)* But the people of the Collective Fruit
Farm Galinsk, their neighbors, propose, instead, that the val-
ley be assigned to them. They would like to plant vineyards

and orchards there. Representing the Reconstruction Commission, I request that these two collective farms decide between themselves whether the Rosa Luxemburg should return here or not.

OLD MAN, *right*: First of all, I want to protest against the time limit on discussion. We of The "Rosa Luxemburg" have spent three days and three nights getting here. And now discussion is limited to half a day!

WOUNDED SOLDIER, *left*: Comrade, we haven't as many villages as we used to have. We haven't as many hands. We haven't as much time.

GIRL TRACTORIST: All pleasures have to be rationed. Tobacco is rationed, and wine. Discussion should be rationed.

OLD MAN, *right (sighing)*: Death to the fascists! All right, I will come to the point and explain just why we want our valley back. Makina Abakidze, unpack the goat cheese. *(A PEASANT WOMAN from the right takes from a basket an enormous cheese wrapped in a cloth. Applause and laughter.)* Help yourselves, Comrades, have some!

OLD MAN, *left (suspiciously)*: Is this a way of influencing us?

OLD MAN, *right (amid laughter)*: How could it be a way of influencing you, Surab, you valley-thief? Everyone knows you'll take the cheese and the valley, too. *(Laughter.)* All I expect from you is an honest answer. Do you like the cheese?

OLD MAN, *left*: The answer is: yes.

OLD MAN, *right*: Really. *(Bitterly)* I might have known you knew nothing about cheese.

OLD MAN, *left*: Why? When I tell you I like it?

OLD MAN, *right*: Because you can't like it. Because it's not what it was in the old days. And why not? Because our goats don't like the new grass. The grazing land over there is no good, whatever the young folks say. You can't live there. It doesn't even smell of morning in the morning. *(Several people laugh.)* Please put that in your report.

DELEGATE: Don't mind them: they got your point. After all, why does a man love his country? Because the bread tastes better there, the air smells better, voices sound stronger, the sky is higher, the ground is easier to walk on. Isn't that so?

OLD MAN, *right*: The valley has belonged to us from all eternity.

SOLDIER, *left*: What does that mean — from all eternity? Nothing belongs to anyone from all eternity. When you were young you didn't even belong to yourself. You belonged to the Kazbeki princes.

OLD MAN, *right*: The valley belongs to us by law.

GIRL TRACTORIST: In any case, the laws must be reexamined to see if they're still right.

OLD MAN, *right*: That goes without saying. But doesn't it make a difference what kind of trees stand next to the house you are born in? Or what kind of neighbors you have? We want to come back just to have you as our neighbors, valley-thieves! Now you can all laugh again.

OLD MAN, *left (laughing)*: Then why don't you listen to what your neighbor, Kato Vachtang, our agriculturist, has to say about the valley?

PEASANT WOMAN, *right*: We've not finished what *we* had to say about this valley. The houses weren't *all* destroyed. As for the dairy farm, at least the foundation's still there.

DELEGATE: If your new grazing land is as bad as all that, you have a good claim to State support.

PEASANT WOMAN, *right*: Comrade Specialist, we're not horse trading. I can't take your cap, hand you another, and say, This one's better. It may be better, but you prefer your own.

GIRL TRACTORIST: A piece of land is not a cap — not in our country, Comrade.

DELEGATE: Don't get angry. It's true a piece of land is a tool to produce something useful, but there's also such a thing as love for a particular piece of land. In any event, what we need to know is exactly what you people would do with the valley if you had it. *(To those on the left.)*

OTHERS: Yes, let Kato speak.

KATO *(rising; she's in military uniform)*: Comrades, last winter, while we were fighting in these hills as Partisans, we discussed how, once the Germans were expelled, we could build up our fruit culture to ten times its original size. I've prepared a plan for an irrigation project. With a dam across our mountain lake we could water seven hundred acres of infertile land. Our farm could not only grow more fruit, it could support vineyards too. The project, however, would only pay if the disputed valley of the Rosa Luxemburg farm were also included. Here are the calculations. *(She hands* DELEGATE *a briefcase.)*

OLD MAN, *right*: Write into the report that our Collective plans to start a new stud farm.

GIRL TRACTORIST: Comrades, the project was conceived during days and nights when we had to run for cover in the mountains. Often, we hadn't even enough ammunition for our half-dozen rifles. We could hardly lay our hands on a pencil. *(Applause from both sides.)*

OLD MAN, *right*: Many thanks to our Comrades of the "Galinsk" and all who have defended our country! *(They shake hands and embrace.)*

GIRL TRACTORIST: As the poet Mayakovsky said: "The home of the Soviet people shall also be the home of Reason!"

*The* DELEGATES *except for the* OLD MAN *have got up, and with the* DELEGATE SPECIFIED *proceed to study the Agriculturist's drawings. Exclamations such as: "Why is the altitude of fall twenty-two meters?"— "This rock must be blown up"— "Actually, all they need is cement and dynamite"— "They force the water to come down here, that's clever!"*

A VERY YOUNG WORKER, *right (to* OLD MAN, *right)*: They're going to irrigate all the fields between the hills, look at that, Aleko!

OLD MAN, *right*: I won't look! I knew the project would be good. I refuse to have a pistol pointed at me!

DELEGATE: But they only want to point a pencil at you! (*Laughter.*)

PEASANT WOMAN, *right*: Aleko Bereshwili, you have a weakness for new projects.

DELEGATE: Comrades, may I report that you all agree to give up the valley?

PEASANT WOMAN, *right*: I agree. What about you, Aleko?

OLD MAN, *right (bent over drawings)*: I move that you let us have copies of the blueprints.

PEASANT WOMAN, *right*: Then we can eat. Once he can talk about blueprints, it's settled. And that goes for the rest of us. (DELEGATES *laughingly embrace again.*)

OLD MAN, *left*: Long live the "Rosa Luxemburg" and much luck to your stud farm!

PEASANT WOMAN, *left*: Comrades, in honor of our guests this evening we are all going to hear the Singer Arkadi Tscheidse. (*Applause.*)

GIRL TRACTORIST *has gone off to bring the* SINGER.

PEASANT WOMAN, *right*: Your entertainment had better be good. It's costing us a valley.

PEASANT WOMAN, *left*: Arkadi has promised to sing something that has a bearing on our problem. He knows twenty-one thousand lines of verse by heart.

OLD MAN, *left*: He's hard to get. The Planning Commission should persuade him to come north more often, Comrade.

DELEGATE: We are more interested in economics, I'm afraid.

OLD MAN, *left (smiling)*: You redistribute vines and tractors, why not songs?

*Enter the* SINGER Arkadi Tscheidse, *led by* GIRL TRACTORIST. *He is a well-built man of simple manners, accompanied by* FOUR MUSICIANS *with their instruments. The artists are greeted with applause.*

GIRL TRACTORIST: The Comrade Specialist, Arkadi.

*The* SINGER *greets them all.*

DELEGATE: It's an honor to meet you. I heard about your songs when I was still at school. Will it be one of the old legends?

THE SINGER: A very old one. It's called The Chalk Circle and comes from the Chinese. But we'll do it, of course, in a changed version. Comrades, we hope you'll find that old poetry can sound well in the shadow of new tractors. It may be a mistake to mix different wines but old and new wisdom mix admirably. Do we get something to eat before the performance?

VOICES: Of course. Everyone into the Club House!

*While everyone begins to move,* DELEGATE *turns to* GIRL TRACTORIST.

DELEGATE: I hope it won't take long. I've got to get back tonight.

GIRL TRACTORIST: How long will it last, Arkadi? The Comrade Specialist must get back to Tiflis tonight.

THE SINGER *(casually)*: It's actually two stories. A couple of hours.

DELEGATE *(confidentially)*: Couldn't you make it shorter?

THE SINGER: No.

*And they all go happily to eat.*

# 1
# The Noble Child

*As the lights go up, the* SINGER *is seen sitting on the floor, a black sheepskin cloak round his shoulders, and a little, well-thumbed notebook in his hand. A small group of listeners—the chorus—sits with him. The manner of his recitation makes it clear that he has told his story over and over again. He mechanically fingers the pages, seldom looking at them. With appropriate gestures, he gives the signal for each scene to begin.*

SINGER:
  In olden times, in a bloody time,
  There ruled in a Caucasian city—
  Men called it City of the Damned—
  A Governor.
  His name was Georgi Abashwili.
  He was rich as Croesus
  He had a beautiful wife
  He had a healthy baby.
  No other governor in Grusinia

Had so many horses in his stable
So many beggars on his doorstep
So many soldiers in his service
So many petitioners in his courtyard.
Georgi Abashwili — how shall I describe him to you?
He enjoyed his life.
On the morning of Easter Sunday
The Governor and his family went to church.
*At the left a large doorway, at the right an even larger gateway.*
BEGGARS *and* PETITIONERS *pour from the gateway, holding up thin* CHILDREN, *crutches, and petitions. They are followed by* IRONSHIRTS, *and then, expensively dressed, the* GOVERNOR'S FAMILY.

BEGGARS AND PETITIONERS:
— Mercy! Mercy, Your Grace! The taxes are too high.
— I lost my leg in the Persian War, where can I get . . .
— My brother is innocent, Your Grace, a misunderstanding . . .
— The child is starving in my arms!
— Our petition is for our son's discharge from the army, our last remaining son!
— Please, Your Grace, the water inspector takes bribes.

*One servant collects the petitions. Another distributes coins from a purse. Soldiers push the crowd back, lashing at them with thick leather whips.*

SOLDIER: Get back! Clear the church door!

*Behind the* GOVERNOR, *his* WIFE, *and the* ADJUTANT, *the* GOVERNOR'S CHILD *is brought through the gateway in an ornate carriage.*

CROWD:
— The baby!
— I can't see it, don't shove so hard!
— God bless the child, Your Grace!

SINGER *(while the crowd is driven back with whips)*:

For the first time on that Easter Sunday, the people saw the
Governor's heir.
Two doctors never moved from the noble child, apple of the
Governor's eye.
Even the mighty Prince Kazbeki bows before him at the
church door.

*A* FAT PRINCE *steps forward and greets the* FAMILY.

FAT PRINCE: Happy Easter, Natella Abashwili! What a day!
When it was raining last night, I thought to myself, gloomy
holidays! But this morning the sky was gay. I love a gay sky,
a simple heart, Natella Abashwili. And little Michael is a
governor from head to foot! Tititi! *(He tickles the* CHILD.*)*

GOVERNOR'S WIFE: What do you think, Arsen, at last Georgi
has decided to start building the east wing. All those wretched
slums are to be torn down to make room for the garden.

FAT PRINCE: Good news after so much bad! What's the latest
on the war, Brother Georgi? *(The* GOVERNOR *indicates a
lack of interest.)* Strategical retreat, I hear. Well, minor reverses
are to be expected. Sometimes things go well, sometimes not.
Such is war. Doesn't mean a thing, does it?

GOVERNOR'S WIFE: He's coughing. Georgi, did you hear? *(She
speaks sharply to the* DOCTORS, *two dignified men standing
close to the little carriage.)* He's coughing!

FIRST DOCTOR *(to the* SECOND*)*: May I remind you, Niko
Mikadze, that I was against the lukewarm bath? *(To the* GOV-
ERNOR'S WIFE:*)* There's been a little error over warming
the bath water, Your Grace.

SECOND DOCTOR *(equally polite)*: Mika Loladze, I'm afraid
I can't agree with you. The temperature of the bath water
was exactly what our great, beloved Mishiko Oboladze pre-
scribed. More likely a slight draft during the night, Your
Grace.

GOVERNOR'S WIFE: But do pay more attention to him. He
looks feverish, Georgi.

FIRST DOCTOR *(bending over the* CHILD*)*: No cause for alarm, Your Grace. The bath water will be warmer. It won't occur again.

SECOND DOCTOR *(with a venomous glance at the* FIRST*)*: I won't forget that, my dear Mika Loladze. No cause for concern, Your Grace.

FAT PRINCE: Well, well, well! I always say: "A pain in my liver? Then the doctor gets fifty strokes on the soles of his feet." We live in a decadent age. In the old days one said: "Off with his head!"

GOVERNOR'S WIFE: Let's go into church. Very likely it's the draft here.

*The procession of* FAMILY *and* SERVANTS *turns into the doorway. The* FAT PRINCE *follows, but the* GOVERNOR *is kept back by the* ADJUTANT, *a handsome young man. When the crowd of* PETITIONERS *has been driven off, a young dust-stained* RIDER, *his arm in a sling, remains behind.*

ADJUTANT *(pointing at the* RIDER, *who steps forward)*: Won't you hear the messenger from the capital, Your Excellency? He arrived this morning. With confidential papers.

GOVERNOR: Not before Service, Shalva. But did you hear Brother Kazbeki wish me a happy Easter? Which is all very well, but I don't believe it did rain last night.

ADJUTANT *(nodding)*: We must investigate.

GOVERNOR: Yes, at once. Tomorrow.

*They pass through the doorway. The* RIDER, *who has waited in vain for an audience, turns sharply round and, muttering a curse, goes off. Only one of the palace guards —* SIMON SHASHAVA *— remains at the door.*

SINGER:
The city is still.
Pigeons strut in the church square.
A soldier of the Palace Guard
Is joking with a kitchen maid
As she comes up from the river with a bundle.

*A girl*—GRUSHA VASHNADZE—*comes through the gateway with a bundle made of large green leaves under her arm.*

SIMON: What, the young lady is not in church? Shirking?

GRUSHA: I was dressed to go. But they needed another goose for the banquet. And they asked me to get it. I know about geese.

SIMON: A goose? *(He feigns suspicion.)* I'd like to see that goose. *(*GRUSHA *does not understand.)* One must be on one's guard with women. "I only went for a fish," they tell you, but it turns out to be something else.

GRUSHA *(walking resolutely toward him and showing him the goose)*: There! If it isn't a fifteen-pound goose stuffed full of corn, I'll eat the feathers.

SIMON: A queen of a goose! The Governor himself will eat it. So the young lady has been down to the river again?

GRUSHA: Yes, at the poultry farm.

SIMON: Really? At the poultry farm, down by the river... not higher up maybe? Near those willows?

GRUSHA: I only go to the willows to wash the linen.

SIMON *(insinuatingly)*: Exactly.

GRUSHA: Exactly what?

SIMON *(winking)*: Exactly that.

GRUSHA: Why shouldn't I wash the linen by the willows?

SIMON *(with exaggerated laughter)*: "Why shouldn't I wash the linen by the willows!" That's good, really good!

GRUSHA: I don't understand the soldier. What's so good about it?

SIMON *(slyly)*: "If something I know someone learns, she'll grow hot and cold by turns!"

GRUSHA: I don't know what I could learn about those willows.

SIMON: Not even if there was a bush opposite? That one could see everything from? Everything that goes on there when a certain person is — "washing linen"?

GRUSHA: What does go on? Won't the soldier say what he means and have done?

SIMON: Something goes on. Something can be seen.

GRUSHA: Could the soldier mean I dip my toes in the water when it's hot? There's nothing else.

SIMON: There's more. Your toes. And more.

GRUSHA: More what? At most my foot?

SIMON: Your foot. And a little more. *(He laughs heartily.)*

GRUSHA *(angrily)*: Simon Shashava, you ought to be ashamed of yourself! To sit in a bush on a hot day and wait till a girl comes and dips her legs in the river! And I bet you bring a friend along too! *(She runs off.)*

SIMON *(shouting after her)*: I didn't bring any friend along!

*As the* SINGER *resumes his tale, the* SOLDIER *steps into the doorway as though to listen to the service.*

SINGER:

The city is still
But why are there armed men?
The Governor's palace is at peace
But why is it a fortress?
And the Governor returned to his palace
And the fortress was a trap
And the goose was plucked and roasted
But the goose was not eaten this time
And noon was no longer the hour to eat:
Noon was the hour to die.

*From the doorway at the left the* FAT PRINCE *quickly appears, stands still, looks around. Before the gateway at the right two* IRONSHIRTS *are squatting and playing dice. The* FAT PRINCE *sees them, walks slowly past, making a sign to them. They rise: one goes through the gateway, the other goes off at the right. Muffled voices are heard from various directions in the rear:* "To your posts!" *The palace is surrounded. The* FAT PRINCE *quickly goes off. Church bells in the distance. Enter, through the doorway, the Governor's family and procession, returning from church.*

GOVERNOR'S WIFE *(passing the* ADJUTANT*)*: It's impossible to live in such a slum. But Georgi, of course, will only build for his little Michael. Never for me! Michael is all! All for Michael!

*The procession turns into the gateway. Again the* ADJUTANT *lingers behind. He waits. Enter the wounded* RIDER *from the doorway. Two* IRONSHIRTS *of the Palace Guard have taken up positions by the gateway.*

ADJUTANT *(to the* RIDER*):* The Governor does not wish to receive military news before dinner—especially if it's depressing, as I assume. In the afternoon His Excellency will confer with prominent architects. They're coming to dinner too. And here they are! *(Enter three gentlemen through the doorway.)* Go to the kitchen and eat, my friend. *(As the* RIDER *goes, the* ADJUTANT *greets the* ARCHITECTS.*)* Gentlemen, His Excellency expects you at dinner. He will devote all his time to you and your great new plans. Come!

ONE OF THE ARCHITECTS: We marvel that His Excellency intends to build. There are disquieting rumors that the war in Persia has taken a turn for the worse.

ADJUTANT: All the more reason to build! There's nothing to those rumors anyway. Persia is a long way off, and the garrison here would let itself be hacked to bits for its Governor. *(Noise from the palace. The shrill scream of a woman. Someone is shouting orders. Dumbfounded, the* ADJUTANT *moves toward the gateway. An* IRONSHIRT *steps out, points his lance at him.)* What's this? Put down that lance, you dog.

ONE OF THE ARCHITECTS: It's the Princes! Don't you know the Princes met last night in the capital? And they're against the Grand Duke and his Governors? Gentlemen, we'd better make ourselves scarce. *(They rush off. The* ADJUTANT *remains helplessly behind.)*

ADJUTANT *(furiously to the Palace Guard):* Down with those lances! Don't you see the Governor's life is threatened?

*The* IRONSHIRTS *of the Palace Guard refuse to obey. They stare coldly and indifferently at the* ADJUTANT *and follow the next events without interest.*

SINGER:

O blindness of the great!
They go their way like gods,
Great over bent backs,
Sure of hired fists,
Trusting in the power
Which has lasted so long.
But long is not forever.
O change from age to age!
Thou hope of the people!

*Enter the* GOVERNOR, *through the gateway, between two* SOL-
DIERS *armed to the teeth. He is in chains. His face is gray.*

Up, great sir, deign to walk upright!
From your palace the eyes of many foes follow you!
And now you don't need an architect, a carpenter will do.
You won't be moving into a new palace
But into a little hole in the ground.
Look about you once more, blind man!

*The arrested man looks round.*

Does all you had please you?
Between the Easter Mass and the Easter meal
You are walking to a place whence no one returns.

*The* GOVERNOR *is led off. A horn sounds an alarm. Noise behind the gateway.*

When the house of a great one collapses
Many little ones are slain.
Those who had no share in the *good* fortunes of the mighty
Often have a share in their *mis*fortunes.
The plunging wagon
Drags the sweating oxen down with it
Into the abyss.

*The* SERVANTS *come rushing through the gateway in panic.*

SERVANTS (*among themselves*):

— The baskets!
— Take them all into the third courtyard! Food for five days!

—The mistress has fainted! Someone must carry her down.

—She must get away.

—What about us? We'll be slaughtered like chickens, as always.

—Goodness, what'll happen? There's bloodshed already in the city, they say.

—Nonsense, the Governor has just been asked to appear at a Princes' meeting. All very correct. Everything'll be ironed out. I heard this on the best authority...

*The two* DOCTORS *rush into the courtyard.*

FIRST DOCTOR *(trying to restrain the other)*: Niko Mikadze, it is your duty as a doctor to attend Natella Abashwili.

SECOND DOCTOR: My duty! It's yours!

FIRST DOCTOR: Whose turn is it to look after the child today, Niko Mikadze, yours or mine?

SECOND DOCTOR: Do you really think, Mika Loladze, I'm going to stay a minute longer in this accursed house on that little brat's account? *(They start fighting. All one hears is:* "You neglect your duty!" *and* "Duty, my foot!" *Then the* SECOND DOCTOR *knocks the* FIRST *down.)* Go to hell! *(Exit.)*

*Enter the soldier,* SIMON SHASHAVA. *He searches in the crowd for* GRUSHA.

SIMON: Grusha! There you are at last! What are you going to do?

GRUSHA: Nothing. If worst comes to worst, I've a brother in the mountains. How about you?

SIMON: Forget about me. *(Formally again:)* Grusha Vashnadze, your wish to know my plans fills me with satisfaction. I've been ordered to accompany Madam Abashwili as her guard.

GRUSHA: But hasn't the Palace Guard mutinied?

SIMON *(seriously)*: That's a fact.

GRUSHA: Isn't it dangerous to go with her?

SIMON: In Tiflis, they say: Isn't the stabbing dangerous for the knife?

GRUSHA: You're not a knife, you're a man, Simon Shashava, what has that woman to do with you?

SIMON: That woman has nothing to do with me. I have my orders, and I go.

GRUSHA: The soldier is pigheaded: he is running into danger for nothing—nothing at all. I must get into the third courtyard, I'm in a hurry.

SIMON: Since we're both in a hurry we shouldn't quarrel. You need time for a good quarrel. May I ask if the young lady still has parents?

GRUSHA: No, just a brother.

SIMON: As time is short—my second question is this: Is the young lady as healthy as a fish in water?

GRUSHA: I may have a pain in the right shoulder once in a while. Otherwise I'm strong enough for my job. No one has complained. So far.

SIMON: That's well known. When it's Easter Sunday, and the question arises who'll run for the goose all the same, she'll be the one. My third question is this: Is the young lady impatient? Does she want apples in winter?

GRUSHA: Impatient? No. But if a man goes to war without any reason and then no message comes—that's bad.

SIMON: A message will come. And now my final question...

GRUSHA: Simon Shashava, I must get to the third courtyard at once. My answer is yes.

SIMON (*very embarrassed*): Haste, they say, is the wind that blows down the scaffolding. But they also say: The rich don't know what haste is. I'm from...

GRUSHA: Kutsk...

SIMON: The young lady has been inquiring about me? I'm healthy, I have no dependents, I make ten piasters a month, as paymaster twenty piasters, and I'm asking—very sincerely—for your hand.

GRUSHA: Simon Shashava, it suits me well.

SIMON (*taking from his neck a thin chain with a little cross on it*): My mother gave me this cross, Grusha Vashnadze. The chain is silver. Please wear it.

GRUSHA: Many thanks, Simon.

SIMON *(hangs it round her neck)*: It would be better to go to the third courtyard now. Or there'll be difficulties. Anyway, I must harness the horses. The young lady will understand?

GRUSHA: Yes, Simon.

*They stand undecided.*

SIMON: I'll just take the mistress to the troops that have stayed loyal. When the war's over, I'll be back. In two weeks. Or three. I hope my intended won't get tired, awaiting my return.

GRUSHA:
Simon Shashava, I shall wait for you.
Go calmly into battle, soldier
The bloody battle, the bitter battle
From which not everyone returns:
When you return I shall be there.
I shall be waiting for you under the green elm
I shall be waiting for you under the bare elm
I shall wait until the last soldier has returned
And longer
When you come back from the battle
No boots will stand at my door
The pillow beside mine will be empty
And my mouth will be unkissed.
When you return, when you return
You will be able to say: It is just as it was.

SIMON: I thank you, Grusha Vashnadze. And good-bye!

*He bows low before her. She does the same before him. Then she runs quickly off without looking round. Enter the* ADJUTANT *from the gateway.*

ADJUTANT *(harshly)*: Harness the horses to the carriage! Don't stand there doing nothing, scum!

SIMON SHASHAVA *stands to attention and goes off. Two* SERVANTS *crowd from the gateway, bent low under huge trunks. Behind them, supported by her women, stumbles* NATELLA ABASHWILI. *She is followed by a* WOMAN *carrying the* CHILD.

GOVERNOR'S WIFE: I hardly know if my head's still on. Where's Michael? Don't hold him so clumsily. Pile the trunks onto the carriage. No news from the city, Shalva?

ADJUTANT: None. All's quiet so far, but there's not a minute to lose. No room for all those trunks in the carriage. Pick out what you need. *(Exit quickly.)*

GOVERNOR'S WIFE: Only essentials! Quick, open the trunks! I'll tell you what I need. *(The trunks are lowered and opened. She points at some brocade dresses.)* The green one! And, of course, the one with the fur trimming. Where are Niko Mikadze and Mika Loladze? I've suddenly got the most terrible migraine again. It always starts in the temples. *(Enter* GRUSHA.*)* Taking your time, eh? Go and get the hot water bottles this minute! *(*GRUSHA *runs off, returns later with hot water bottles; the* GOVERNOR'S WIFE *orders her about by signs.)* Don't tear the sleeves.

A YOUNG WOMAN: Pardon, madam, no harm has come to the dress.

GOVERNOR'S WIFE: Because I stopped you. I've been watching you for a long time. Nothing in your head but making eyes at Shalva Tzereteli. I'll kill you, you bitch! *(She beats the* YOUNG WOMAN.*)*

ADJUTANT *(appearing in the gateway)*: Please make haste, Natella Abashwili. Firing has broken out in the city. *(Exit.)*

GOVERNOR'S WIFE *(letting go of the* YOUNG WOMAN*)*: Oh dear, do you think they'll lay hands on us? Why should they? Why? *(She herself begins to rummage in the trunks.)* How's Michael? Asleep?

WOMAN WITH THE CHILD: Yes, madam.

GOVERNOR'S WIFE: Then put him down a moment and get my little saffron-colored boots from the bedroom. I need them for the green dress. *(The* WOMAN *puts down the* CHILD *and goes off.)* Just look how these things have been packed! No love! No understanding! If you don't give them every order yourself... At such moments you realize what kind of servants you have! They gorge themselves at your expense, and never a word of gratitude! I'll remember this.

ADJUTANT *(entering, very excited)*: Natella, you must leave at once!

GOVERNOR'S WIFE: Why? I've got to take this silver dress — it cost a thousand piasters. And that one there, and where's the wine-colored one?

ADJUTANT *(trying to pull her away)*: Riots have broken out! We must leave at once. Where's the baby?

GOVERNOR'S WIFE *(calling to the* YOUNG WOMAN *who was holding the baby)*: Maro, get the baby ready! Where on earth are you?

ADJUTANT *(leaving)*: We'll probably have to leave the carriage behind and go ahead on horseback.

*The* GOVERNOR'S WIFE *rummages again among her dresses, throws some onto the heap of chosen clothes, then takes them off again. Noises, drums are heard. The* YOUNG WOMAN *who was beaten creeps away. The sky begins to grow red.*

GOVERNOR'S WIFE *(rummaging desperately)*: I simply cannot find the wine-colored dress. Take the whole pile to the carriage. Where's Asja? And why hasn't Maro come back? Have you all gone crazy?

ADJUTANT *(returning)*: Quick! Quick!

GOVERNOR'S WIFE *(to the* FIRST WOMAN*)*: Run! Just throw them into the carriage!

ADJUTANT: We're not taking the carriage. And if you don't come now, I'll ride off on my own.

GOVERNOR'S WIFE *(as the* FIRST WOMAN *can't carry everything)*: Where's that bitch Asja? *(The* ADJUTANT *pulls her away.)* Maro, bring the baby! *(To the* FIRST WOMAN:*)* Go and look for Masha. No, first take the dresses to the carriage. Such nonsense! I wouldn't dream of going on horseback!

*Turning round, she sees the red sky, and starts back rigid. The fire burns. She is pulled out by the* ADJUTANT. *Shaking, the* FIRST WOMAN *follows with the dresses.*

MARO (*from the doorway with the boots*): Madam! (*She sees the trunks and dresses and runs toward the* CHILD, *picks it up, and holds it a moment.*) They left it behind, the beasts. (*She hands it to* GRUSHA.) Hold it a moment. (*She runs off, following the* GOVERNOR'S WIFE.)
*Enter* SERVANTS *from the gateway.*

COOK: Well, so they've actually gone. Without the food wagons, and not a minute too early. It's time for us to clear out.

GROOM: This'll be an unhealthy neighborhood for quite a while. (*To one of the* WOMEN:) Suliko, take a few blankets and wait for me in the foal stables.

GRUSHA: What have they done with the Governor?

GROOM (*gesturing throat cutting*): Ffffft.

A FAT WOMAN (*seeing the gesture and becoming hysterical*): Oh dear, oh dear, oh dear, oh dear! Our master Georgi Abashwili! A picture of health he was, at the morning Mass — and now! Oh, take me away, we're all lost, we must die in sin like our master, Georgi Abashwili!

OTHER WOMAN (*soothing her*): Calm down, Nina! You'll be taken to safety. You've never hurt a fly.

FAT WOMAN (*being led out*): Oh dear, oh dear, oh dear! Quick! Let's all get out before they come, before they come!

A YOUNG WOMAN: Nina takes it more to heart than the mistress, that's a fact. They even have to have their weeping done for them.

COOK: We'd better get out, all of us.

ANOTHER WOMAN (*glancing back*): That must be the East Gate burning.

YOUNG WOMAN (*seeing the* CHILD *in* GRUSHA's *arms*): The baby! What are you doing with it?

GRUSHA: It got left behind.

YOUNG WOMAN: She simply left it there. Michael, who was kept out of all the drafts!
*The* SERVANTS *gather round the* CHILD.

GRUSHA: He's waking up.

GROOM: Better put him down, I tell you. I'd rather not think what'd happen to anybody who was found with that baby.

COOK: That's right. Once they get started, they'll kill each other off, whole families at a time. Let's go.

*Exeunt all but* GRUSHA, *with the* CHILD *on her arm, and* TWO WOMEN.

TWO WOMEN: Didn't you hear? Better put him down.

GRUSHA: The nurse asked me to hold him a moment.

OLDER WOMAN: She's not coming back, you simpleton.

YOUNGER WOMAN: Keep your hands off it.

OLDER WOMAN *(amiably)*: Grusha, you're a good soul, but you're not very bright, and you know it. I tell you, if he had the plague he couldn't be more dangerous.

GRUSHA *(stubbornly)*: He hasn't got the plague. He looks at me! He's human!

OLDER WOMAN: Don't look at *him*. You're a fool — the kind that always gets put upon. A person need only say, "Run for the salad, you have the longest legs," and you run. My husband has an ox cart — you can come with us if you hurry! Lord, by now the whole neighborhood must be in flames.

*Both women leave, sighing. After some hesitation,* GRUSHA *puts the sleeping* CHILD *down, looks at it for a moment, then takes a brocade blanket from the heap of clothes and covers it. Then both women return, dragging bundles.* GRUSHA *starts guiltily away from the* CHILD *and walks a few steps to one side.*

YOUNGER WOMAN: Haven't you packed anything yet? There isn't much time, you know. The Ironshirts will be here from the barracks.

GRUSHA: Coming!

*She runs through the doorway. Both women go to the gateway and wait. The sound of horses is heard. They flee, screaming. Enter the* FAT PRINCE *with drunken* IRONSHIRTS. *One of them carries the Governor's head on a lance.*

FAT PRINCE: Here! In the middle! *(One soldier climbs onto the other's back, takes the head, holds it tentatively over the door.)*

That's not the middle. Farther to the right. That's it. What I do, my friends, I do well. *(While with hammer and nail, the soldier fastens the head to the wall by its hair.)* This morning at the church door I said to Georgi Abashwili: "I love a gay sky." Actually, I prefer the lightning that comes out of a gay sky. Yes, indeed. It's a pity they took the brat along, though, I need him, urgently.

*Exit with* IRONSHIRTS *through the gateway. Trampling of horses again. Enter* GRUSHA *through the doorway looking cautiously about her. Clearly she has waited for the* IRONSHIRTS *to go. Carrying a bundle, she walks toward the gateway. At the last moment, she turns to see if the* CHILD *is still there. Catching sight of the head over the doorway, she screams. Horrified, she picks up her bundle again, and is about to leave when the* SINGER *starts to speak. She stands rooted to the spot.*

SINGER:

As she was standing between courtyard and gate,
She heard or she thought she heard a low voice calling.
The child called to her,
Not whining, but calling quite sensibly,
Or so it seemed to her.
"Woman," it said, "help me."
And it went on, not whining, but saying quite sensibly:
"Know, woman, he who hears not a cry for help
But passes by with troubled ears will never hear
The gentle call of a lover nor the blackbird at dawn
Nor the happy sigh of the tired grape-picker as the Angelus
   rings."

*She walks a few steps toward the* CHILD *and bends over it.*
Hearing this she went back for one more look at the child:
Only to sit with him for a moment or two,
Only till someone should come,
His mother, or anyone.

*Leaning on a trunk, she sits facing the* CHILD.

Only till she would have to leave, for the danger was too
  great,
The city was full of flame and crying.
*The light grows dimmer, as though evening and night were com-*
*ing on.*
Fearful is the seductive power of goodness!
GRUSHA *now settles down to watch over the* CHILD *through*
*the night. Once, she lights a small lamp to look at it. Once, she*
*tucks it in with a coat. From time to time she listens and looks*
*to see whether someone is coming.*
And she sat with the child a long time,
Till evening came, till night came, till dawn came.
She sat too long, too long she saw
The soft breathing, the small clenched fists,
Till toward morning the seduction was complete
And she rose, and bent down and, sighing, took the child
And carried it away.
*She does what the* SINGER *says as he describes it.*
As if it was stolen goods she picked it up.
As if she was a thief she crept away.

# The Flight into the Northern Mountains

SINGER:
  When Grusha Vashnadze left the city
  On the Grusinian highway
  On the way to the Northern Mountains
  She sang a song, she bought some milk.
CHORUS:
  How will this human child escape
  The bloodhounds, the trap-setters?
  Into the deserted mountains she journeyed
  Along the Grusinian highway she journeyed
  She sang a song, she bought some milk.
  GRUSHA VASHNADZE *walks on. On her back she carries the*
  CHILD *in a sack, in one hand is a large stick, in the other a*
  *bundle. She sings.*

### THE SONG OF THE FOUR GENERALS

  Four generals
  Set out for Iran.
  With the first one, war did not agree.

The second never won a victory.
For the third the weather never was right.
For the fourth the men would never fight.
Four generals
And not a single man!

Sosso Robakidse
Went marching to Iran
With him the war did so agree
He soon had won a victory.
For him the weather was always right.
For him the men would always fight.
Sosso Robakidse,
He is our man!

*A peasant's cottage appears.*

GRUSHA *(to the* CHILD*)*: Noontime is meal time. Now we'll
sit hopefully in the grass, while the good Grusha goes and
buys a little pitcher of milk. *(She lays the* CHILD *down and
knocks at the cottage door. An* OLD MAN *opens it.)* Grandfather, could I have a little pitcher of milk? And a corn cake,
maybe?

OLD MAN: Milk? We have no milk. The soldiers from the city
have our goats. Go to the soldiers if you want milk.

GRUSHA: But grandfather, you must have a little pitcher of
milk for a baby?

OLD MAN: And for a God-bless-you, eh?

GRUSHA: Who said anything about a God-bless-you? *(She shows
her purse.)* We'll pay like princes. "Head in the clouds, backside in the water." *(The peasant goes off, grumbling, for
milk.)* How much for the milk?

OLD MAN: Three piasters. Milk has gone up.

GRUSHA: Three piasters for this little drop? *(Without a word
the* OLD MAN *shuts the door in her face.)* Michael, did you
hear that? Three piasters! We can't afford it! *(She goes back,*

*sits down again, and gives the* CHILD *her breast.)* Suck. Think of the three piasters. There's nothing there, but you *think* you're drinking, and that's something. *(Shaking her head, she sees that the* CHILD *isn't sucking any more. She gets up, walks back to the door, and knocks again.)* Open, grandfather, we'll pay. *(Softly.)* May lightning strike you! *(When the* OLD MAN *appears:)* I thought it would be half a piaster. But the baby must be fed. How about one piaster for that little drop?

OLD MAN: Two.

GRUSHA: Don't shut the door again. *(She fishes a long time in her bag.)* Here are two piasters. The milk better be good. I still have two days' journey ahead of me. It's a murderous business you have here — and sinful, too!

OLD MAN: Kill the soldiers if you want milk.

GRUSHA *(giving the* CHILD *some milk)*: This is an expensive joke. Take a sip, Michael, it's a week's pay. Around here they think we earned our money just sitting on our behinds. Oh, Michael, Michael, you're a nice little load for a girl to take on! *(Uneasy, she gets up, puts the* CHILD *on her back, and walks on. The* OLD MAN, *grumbling, picks up the pitcher and looks after her unmoved.)*

SINGER:
As Grusha Vashnadze went northward
The Princes' Ironshirts went after her.

CHORUS:
How will the barefoot girl escape the Ironshirts,
The bloodhounds, the trap-setters?
They hunt even by night.
Pursuers never tire.
Butchers sleep little.

*Two* IRONSHIRTS *are trudging along the highway.*

CORPORAL: You'll never amount to anything, blockhead, your heart's not in it. Your senior officer sees this in little things. Yesterday, when I made the fat gal, yes, you grabbed her husband as I commanded, and you did kick him in the belly, at my request, but did you *enjoy* it, like a loyal Private, or were you just doing your duty? I've kept an eye on you block-head, you're a hollow reed and a tinkling cymbal, you won't get promoted. *(They walk a while in silence.)* Don't think I've forgotten how insubordinate you are, either. Stop limping! I forbid you to limp! You limp because I sold the horses, and I sold the horses because I'd never have got that price again. You limp to show me you don't like marching. I know you. It won't help. You wait. Sing!

TWO IRONSHIRTS *(singing)*:
Sadly to war I went my way
Leaving my loved one at her door.
My friends will keep her honor safe
Till from the war I'm back once more.

CORPORAL: Louder!

TWO IRONSHIRTS *(singing)*:
When 'neath a headstone I shall be
My love a little earth will bring:
"Here rest the feet that oft would run to me
And here the arms that oft to me would cling."
*They begin to walk again in silence.*

CORPORAL: A good soldier has his heart and soul in it. When he receives an order, he gets a hard-on, and when he drives his lance into the enemy's guts, he comes. *(He shouts for joy.)* He lets himself be torn to bits for his superior officer, and as he lies dying he takes note that his corporal is nodding approval, and that is reward enough, it's his dearest wish. *You* won't get any nod of approval, but you'll croak all right. Christ, how'm I to get my hands on the Governor's bastard with the help of a fool like you! *(They stay on stage behind.)*

SINGER:
When Grusha Vashnadze came to the River Sirra
Flight grew too much for her, the helpless child too heavy.
In the cornfields the rosy dawn
Is cold to the sleepless one, only cold.

The gay clatter of the milk cans in the farmyard where the
  smoke rises
Is only a threat to the fugitive.
She who carries the child feels its weight and little more.
GRUSHA *stops in front of a farm. A fat* PEASANT WOMAN
*is carrying a milk can through the door.* GRUSHA *waits until
she has gone in, then approaches the house cautiously.*
GRUSHA *(to the* CHILD*):* Now you've wet yourself again, and
  you know I've no linen. Michael, this is where we part company. It's far enough from the city. They wouldn't want you
  *so* much that they'd follow you all *this* way, little good-for-
  nothing. The peasant woman is kind, and can't you just smell
  the milk? *(She bends down to lay the* CHILD *on the threshold.)* So farewell, Michael, I'll forget how you kicked me in
  the back all night to make me walk faster. And you can forget
  the meager fare — it was meant well. I'd like to have kept
  you — your nose is so tiny — but it can't be. I'd have shown
  you your first rabbit, I'd have trained you to keep dry, but
  now I must turn around. My sweetheart the soldier might
  be back soon, and suppose he didn't find me? You can't ask
  that, can you? *(She creeps up to the door and lays the* CHILD
  *on the threshold. Then, hiding behind a tree, she waits until
  the* PEASANT WOMAN *opens the door and sees the bundle.)*
PEASANT WOMAN: Good heavens, what's this? Husband!
PEASANT: What is it? Let me finish my soup.
PEASANT WOMAN *(to the* CHILD*):* Where's your mother then?
  Haven't you got one? It's a boy. Fine linen. He's from a good
  family, you can see that. And they just leave him on our
  doorstep. Oh, these are times!
PEASANT: If they think we're going to feed it, they're wrong. You
  can take it to the priest in the village. That's the best we can do.
PEASANT WOMAN: What'll the priest do with him? He needs
  a mother. There, he's waking up. Don't you think we could
  keep him, though?
PEASANT *(shouting):* No!

PEASANT WOMAN: I could lay him in the corner by the arm-chair. All I need is a crib. I can take him into the fields with me. See him laughing? Husband, we have a roof over our heads. We can do it. Not another word out of you!

*She carries the* CHILD *into the house. The* PEASANT *follows protesting.* GRUSHA *steps out from behind the tree, laughs, and hurries off in the opposite direction.*

SINGER:
Why so cheerful, making for home?

CHORUS:
Because the child has won new parents with a laugh,
Because I'm rid of the little one, I'm cheerful.

SINGER:
And why so sad?

CHORUS:
Because I'm single and free, I'm sad
Like someone who's been robbed
Someone who's newly poor.

*She walks for a short while, then meets the two* IRONSHIRTS *who point their lances at her.*

CORPORAL: Lady, you are running straight into the arms of the Armed Forces. Where are you coming from? And when? Are you having illicit relations with the enemy? Where is he hiding? What movements is he making in your rear? How about the hills? How about the valleys? How are your stockings held in position? (GRUSHA *stands there frightened.*) Don't be scared, we always withdraw, if necessary... what, block-head? I always withdraw. In that respect at least, I can be re-lied on. Why are you staring like that at my lance? In the field no soldier drops his lance, that's a rule. Learn it by heart, blockhead. Now, lady, where are you headed?

GRUSHA: To meet my intended, one Simon Shashava, of the Palace Guard in Nuka.

CORPORAL: Simon Shashava? Sure, I know him. He gave me the key so I could look you up once in a while. Blockhead, we are getting to be unpopular. We must make her realize we have honorable intentions. Lady, behind apparent frivolity I conceal a serious nature, so let me tell you officially: I want a child from you. *(GRUSHA utters a little scream.)* Blockhead, she understands me. Uh-huh, isn't it a sweet shock? "Then first I must take the noodles out of the oven, Officer. Then first I must change my torn shirt, Colonel." But away with jokes, away with my lance! We are looking for a baby. A baby from a good family. Have you heard of such a baby, from the city, dressed in fine linen, and suddenly turning up here?

GRUSHA: No, I haven't heard a thing. *(Suddenly she turns round and runs back, panic-stricken. The* IRONSHIRTS *glance at each other, then follow her, cursing.)*

SINGER:
Run, kind girl! The killers are coming!
Help the helpless babe, helpless girl!
And so she runs!

CHORUS:
In the bloodiest times
There are kind people.

*As* GRUSHA *rushes into the cottage, the* PEASANT WOMAN *is bending over the* CHILD's *crib.*

GRUSHA: Hide him. Quick! The Ironshirts are coming! I laid him on your doorstep. But he isn't mine. He's from a good family.

PEASANT WOMAN: Who's coming? What Ironshirts?

GRUSHA: Don't ask questions. The Ironshirts that are looking for it.

PEASANT WOMAN: They've no business in my house. But I must have a little talk with you, it seems.

GRUSHA: Take off the fine linen. It'll give us away.

PEASANT WOMAN: Linen, my foot! In this house I make the decisions! "*You* can't vomit in *my* room!" Why did you abandon it? It's a sin.

GRUSHA *(looking out of the window)*: Look, they're coming out from behind those trees! I shouldn't have run away, it made them angry. Oh, what shall I do?

PEASANT WOMAN *(looking out of the window and suddenly starting with fear)*: Gracious! Ironshirts!

GRUSHA: They're after the baby.

PEASANT WOMAN: Suppose they come in!

GRUSHA: You mustn't give him to them. Say he's yours.

PEASANT WOMAN: Yes.

GRUSHA: They'll run him through if you hand him over.

PEASANT WOMAN: But suppose they ask for it? The silver for the harvest is in the house.

GRUSHA: If you let them have him, they'll run him through, right here in this room! You've got to say he's yours!

PEASANT WOMAN: Yes. But what if they don't believe me?

GRUSHA: You must be firm.

PEASANT WOMAN: They'll burn the roof over our heads.

GRUSHA: That's why you must say he's yours. His name's Michael. But I shouldn't have told you. *(The* PEASANT WOMAN *nods.)* Don't nod like that. And don't tremble—they'll notice.

PEASANT WOMAN: Yes.

GRUSHA: And stop saying yes, I can't stand it. *(She shakes the* WOMAN.*)* Don't you have any children?

PEASANT WOMAN *(muttering)*: He's in the war.

GRUSHA: Then maybe *he's* an Ironshirt? Do you want *him* to run children through with a lance? You'd bawl him out. "No fooling with lances in my house!" you'd shout, "is that what I've reared you for? Wash your neck before you speak to your mother!"

PEASANT WOMAN: That's true, he couldn't get away with anything around here!

GRUSHA: So you'll say he's yours?

PEASANT WOMAN: Yes.

GRUSHA: Look! They're coming!

*There is a knocking at the door. The women don't answer. En-ter* IRONSHIRTS. *The* PEASANT WOMAN *bows low.*

CORPORAL: Well, here she is. What did I tell you? What a nose I have! I *smelt* her. Lady, I have a question for you. Why did you run away? What did you think I would do to you? I'll bet it was something unchaste. Confess!

GRUSHA *(while the* PEASANT WOMAN *bows again and again.)*: I'd left some milk on the stove, and I suddenly remembered it.

CORPORAL: Or maybe you imagined I looked at you unchaste-ly? Like there could be something between us? A carnal glance, know what I mean?

GRUSHA: I didn't see it.

CORPORAL: But it's possible, huh? You admit that much. Af-ter all, I might be a pig. I'll be frank with you: I could think of all sorts of things if we were alone. *(To the* PEASANT WOMAN:*)* Shouldn't you be busy in the yard? Feeding the hens?

PEASANT WOMAN *(falling suddenly to her knees)*: Soldier, I didn't know a thing about it. Please don't burn the roof over our heads.

CORPORAL: What are you talking about?

PEASANT WOMAN: I had nothing to do with it. She left it on my doorstep, I swear it!

CORPORAL *(suddenly seeing the* CHILD *and whistling)*: Ah, so there's a little something in the crib! Blockhead, I smell a thousand piasters. Take the old girl outside and hold on to her. It looks like I have a little cross-examining to do. *(The* PEASANT WOMAN *lets herself be led out by the* PRIVATE, *without a word.)* So, you've *got* the child I wanted from you! *(He walks toward the crib.)*

GRUSHA: Officer, he's mine. He's not the one you're after.

CORPORAL: I'll just take a look. *(He bends over the crib.)*

GRUSHA *looks round in despair.*

GRUSHA: He's mine! He's mine!

CORPORAL: Fine linen!

GRUSHA *dashes at him to pull him away. He throws her off and again bends over the crib. Again looking round in despair, she sees a log of wood, seizes it, and hits the* CORPORAL *over the head from behind. The* CORPORAL *collapses. She quickly picks up the* CHILD *and rushes off.*

SINGER:

And in her flight from the Ironshirts
After twenty-two days of journeying
At the foot of the Janga-Tau Glacier
Grusha Vashnadze decided to adopt the child.

CHORUS:

The helpless girl adopted the helpless child.

GRUSHA *squats over a half-frozen stream to get the* CHILD *water in the hollow of her hand.*

GRUSHA:

Since no one else will take you, son,
I must take you.
Since no one else will take you, son,
You must take me.
O black day in a lean, lean year,
The trip was long, the milk was dear,
My legs are tired, my feet are sore:
But I wouldn't be without you any more.
I'll throw your silken shirt away
And wrap you in rags and tatters.
I'll wash you, son, and christen you in glacier water.
We'll see it through together.
*She has taken off the child's fine linen and wrapped it in a rag.*

SINGER:

When Grusha Vashnadze
Pursued by the Ironshirts
Came to the bridge on the glacier
Leading to the villages of the Eastern Slope
She sang the Song of the Rotten Bridge
And risked two lives.

*A wind has risen. The bridge on the glacier is visible in the dark. One rope is broken and half the bridge is hanging down the abyss.* MERCHANTS, *two men and a woman, stand undecided before the bridge as* GRUSHA *and the* CHILD *arrive. One man is trying to catch the hanging rope with a stick.*

FIRST MAN: Take your time, young woman. You won't get across here anyway.

GRUSHA: But I *have* to get the baby to the east side. To my brother's place.

MERCHANT WOMAN: Have to? How d'you mean, "have to"? I have to get there, too — because I have to buy carpets in Atum — carpets a woman had to sell because her husband had to die. But can *I* do what I have to? Can she? Andrei's been fishing for that rope for hours. And I ask you, how are we going to fasten it, even if he gets it up?

FIRST MAN *(listening)*: Hush, I think I hear something.

GRUSHA: The bridge isn't quite rotted through. I think I'll try it.

MERCHANT WOMAN: *I* wouldn't — if the devil himself were after me. It's suicide.

FIRST MAN *(shouting)*: Hi!

GRUSHA: Don't shout! *(To the* MERCHANT WOMAN:*)* Tell him not to shout.

FIRST MAN: But there's someone down there calling. Maybe they've lost their way.

MERCHANT WOMAN: Why shouldn't he shout? Is there something funny about you? Are they after you?

GRUSHA: All right, I'll tell. The Ironshirts are after me. I knocked one down.

SECOND MAN: Hide our merchandise!

*The* WOMAN *hides a sack behind a rock.*

FIRST MAN: Why didn't you say so right away? *(To the others:)* If they catch her they'll make mincemeat out of her!

GRUSHA: Get out of my way. I've got to cross that bridge.

SECOND MAN: You can't. The precipice is two thousand feet deep.

FIRST MAN: Even with the rope it'd be no use. We could hold it up with our hands. But then we'd have to do the same for the Ironshirts.

GRUSHA: Go away.

*There are calls from the distance:* "Hi, up there!"

MERCHANT WOMAN: They're getting near. But you can't take the child on that bridge. It's sure to break. And look!

GRUSHA *looks down into the abyss. The* IRONSHIRTS *are heard calling again from below.*

SECOND MAN: Two thousand feet!

GRUSHA: But those men are worse.

FIRST MAN: You can't do it. Think of the baby. Risk your life but not a child's.

SECOND MAN: With the child she's that much heavier!

MERCHANT WOMAN: Maybe she's *really* got to get across. Give *me* the baby. I'll hide it. Cross the bridge alone!

GRUSHA: I won't. We belong together. *(To the* CHILD:*)* "Live together, die together." *(She sings.)*

THE SONG OF THE ROTTEN BRIDGE

> Deep is the abyss, son,
> I see the weak bridge sway
> But it's not for us, son,
> To choose the way.
>
> The way I know
> Is the one you must tread,
> And all you will eat
> Is my bit of bread.
>
> Of every four pieces
> You shall have three.

> Would that I knew
> How big they will be!

Get out of my way, I'll try it without the rope.

MERCHANT WOMAN: You are tempting God!

*There are shouts from below.*

GRUSHA: Please, throw that stick away, or they'll get the rope and follow me. (*Pressing the* CHILD *to her, she steps onto the swaying bridge. The* MERCHANT WOMAN *screams when it looks as though the bridge is about to collapse. But* GRUSHA *walks on and reaches the far side.*)

FIRST MAN: She made it!

MERCHANT WOMAN (*who has fallen on her knees and begun to pray, angrily*): I still think it was a sin.

*The* IRONSHIRTS *appear; the* CORPORAL's *head is bandaged.*

CORPORAL: Seen a woman with a child?

FIRST MAN (*while the* SECOND MAN *throws the stick into the abyss*): Yes, there! But the bridge won't carry you!

CORPORAL: You'll pay for this, blockhead!

GRUSHA, *from the far bank, laughs and shows the* CHILD *to the* IRONSHIRTS. *She walks on. The wind blows.*

GRUSHA (*turning to the* CHILD): You mustn't be afraid of the wind. He's a poor thing too. He has to push the clouds along and he gets quite cold doing it. (*Snow starts falling.*) And the snow isn't so bad, either, Michael. It covers the little fir trees so they won't die in winter. Let me sing you a little song. (*She sings.*)

### THE SONG OF THE CHILD

> Your father is a bandit
> A harlot the mother who bore you.
> Yet honorable men
> Shall kneel down before you.

Food to the baby horses
The tiger's son will take.
The mothers will get milk
From the son of the snake.

## 3

# In the Northern Mountains

SINGER:
> Seven days the sister, Grusha Vashnadze,
> Journeyed across the glacier
> And down the slopes she journeyed.
> "When I enter my brother's house," she thought,
> "He will rise and embrace me."
> "Is that you, sister?" he will say,
> "I have long expected you.
> This is my dear wife,
> And this is my farm, come to me by marriage,
> With eleven horses and thirty-one cows. Sit down.
> Sit down with your child at our table and eat."
> The brother's house was in a lovely valley.
> When the sister came to the brother,
> She was ill from walking.
> The brother rose from the table.

*A fat peasant couple rise from the table.* LAVRENTI VASH-
NADZE *still has a napkin round his neck, as* GRUSHA, *pale
and supported by a* SERVANT, *enters with the* CHILD.
LAVRENTI: Where've *you* come from, Grusha?

GRUSHA *(feebly)*: Across the Janga-Tu Pass, Lavrenti.

SERVANT: I found her in front of the hay barn. She has a baby with her.

SISTER-IN-LAW: Go and groom the mare.

*Exit the* SERVANT.

LAVRENTI: This is my wife Aniko.

SISTER-IN-LAW: I thought you were in service in Nuka.

GRUSHA *(barely able to stand)*: Yes, I was.

SISTER-IN-LAW: Wasn't it a good job? We were told it was.

GRUSHA: The Governor got killed.

LAVRENTI: Yes, we heard there were riots. Your aunt told us. Remember, Aniko?

SISTER-IN-LAW: Here with us, it's very quiet. City people always want something going on. *(She walks toward the door, calling:)* Sosso, Sosso, don't take the cake out of the oven yet, d'you hear? Where on earth are you? *(Exit, calling.)*

LAVRENTI *(quietly, quickly)*: Is there a father? *(As she shakes her head:)* I thought not. We must think up something. She's religious.

SISTER-IN-LAW *(returning)*: Those servants! *(To* GRUSHA:*)* You have a child.

GRUSHA: It's mine. *(She collapses.* LAVRENTI *rushes to her assistance.)*

SISTER-IN-LAW: Heavens, she's ill — what are we going to do?

LAVRENTI *(escorting her to a bench near the stove)*: Sit down, sit. I think it's just weakness, Aniko.

SISTER-IN-LAW: As long as it's not scarlet fever!

LAVRENTI: She'd have spots if it was. It's only weakness. Don't worry, Aniko. *(To* GRUSHA:*)* Better, sitting down?

SISTER-IN-LAW: Is the child hers?

GRUSHA: Yes, mine.

LAVRENTI: She's on her way to her husband.

SISTER-IN-LAW: I see. Your meat's getting cold. *(*LAVRENTI *sits down and begins to eat.)* Cold food's not good for you, the fat mustn't get cold, you know your stomach's your weak spot. *(To* GRUSHA:*)* If your husband's not in the city, where is he?

LAVRENTI: She got married on the other side of the mountain, she says.

SISTER-IN-LAW: On the other side of the mountain. I see. *(She also sits down to eat.)*

GRUSHA: I think I should lie down somewhere, Lavrenti.

SISTER-IN-LAW: If it's consumption we'll all get it. *(She goes on cross-examining her.)* Has your husband got a farm?

GRUSHA: He's a soldier.

LAVRENTI: But he's coming into a farm — a small one — from his father.

SISTER-IN-LAW: Isn't he in the war? Why not?

GRUSHA *(with effort)*: Yes, he's in the war.

SISTER-IN-LAW: Then why d'you want to go to the farm?

LAVRENTI: When he comes back from the war, he'll return to his farm.

SISTER-IN-LAW: But you're going there now?

LAVRENTI: Yes, to wait for him.

SISTER-IN-LAW *(calling shrilly)*: Sosso, the cake!

GRUSHA *(murmuring feverishly)*: A farm — a soldier — waiting — sit down, eat.

SISTER-IN-LAW: It's scarlet fever.

GRUSHA *(starting up)*: Yes, he's got a farm!

LAVRENTI: I think it's just weakness, Aniko. Would you look after the cake yourself, dear?

SISTER-IN-LAW: But when will he come back if war's broken out again as people say? *(She waddles off, shouting.)* Sosso! Where on earth are you? Sosso!

LAVRENTI *(getting up quickly and going to* GRUSHA*)*: You'll get a bed in a minute. She has a good heart. But wait till after supper.

GRUSHA *(holding out the* CHILD *to him)*: Take him.

LAVRENTI *(taking it and looking around)*: But you can't stay here long with the child. She's religious, you see.

GRUSHA *collapses.* LAVRENTI *catches her.*

SINGER:

The sister was so ill,
The cowardly brother had to give her shelter.
Summer departed, winter came.
The winter was long, the winter was short.
People mustn't know anything.
Rats mustn't bite.
Spring mustn't come.

GRUSHA *sits over the weaving loom in a workroom. She and the* CHILD, *who is squatting on the floor, are wrapped in blankets. She sings.*

### THE SONG OF THE CENTER

And the lover started to leave
And his betrothed ran pleading after him
Pleading and weeping, weeping and teaching:
"Dearest mine, dearest mine
When you go to war as now you do
When you fight the foe as soon you will
Don't lead with the front line
And don't push with the rear line
At the front is red fire
In the rear is red smoke
Stay in the war's center
Stay near the standard bearer
The first always die
The last are also hit
Those in the center come home."

Michael, we must be clever. If we make ourselves as small as
cockroaches, the sister-in-law will forget we're in the house,
and then we can stay till the snow melts.

*Enter* LAVRENTI. *He sits down beside his sister.*

LAVRENTI: Why are you sitting there muffled up like coachmen, you two? Is it too cold in the room?

GRUSHA *(hastily removing one shawl)*: It's not too cold, Lavrenti.

LAVRENTI: If it's too cold, you shouldn't be sitting here with the child. Aniko would never forgive herself! *(Pause.)* I hope our priest didn't question you about the child?

GRUSHA: He did, but I didn't tell him anything.

LAVRENTI: That's good. I wanted to speak to you about Aniko. She has a good heart but she's very, very sensitive. People need only mention our farm and she's worried. She takes everything hard, you see. One time our milkmaid went to church with a hole in her stocking. Ever since, Aniko has worn two pairs of stockings in church. It's the old family in her. *(He listens.)* Are you sure there are no rats around? If there are rats, you couldn't live here. *(There are sounds as of dripping from the roof.)* What's that, dripping?

GRUSHA: It must be a barrel leaking.

LAVRENTI: Yes, it must be a barrel. You've been here six months, haven't you? Was I talking about Aniko? *(They listen again to the snow melting.)* You can't imagine how worried she gets about your soldier-husband. "Suppose he comes back and can't find her!" she says and lies awake. "He can't come before the spring," I tell her. The dear woman! *(The drops begin to fall faster.)* When d'you think he'll come? What do *you* think? (GRUSHA *is silent.*) Not before the spring, you agree? (GRUSHA *is silent.*) You don't believe he'll come at all? (GRUSHA *is silent.*) But when the spring comes and the snow melts here and on the passes, you can't stay on. They may come and look for you. There's already talk of an illegitimate child. *(The "glockenspiel" of the falling drops has grown faster and steadier.)* Grusha, the snow is melting on the roof. Spring is here.

GRUSHA: Yes.

LAVRENTI *(eagerly)*: I'll tell you what we'll do. You need a place to go, and, because of the child *(he sighs)*, you have to have a husband, so people won't talk. Now I've made cautious inquiries to see if we can find you a husband. Grusha, I *have* one. I talked to a peasant woman who has a son. Just the other side of the mountain. A small farm. And she's willing.

GRUSHA: But I *can't* marry! I must wait for Simon Shashava.

LAVRENTI: Of course. That's all been taken care of. You don't need a man in bed—you need a man on paper. And I've found you one. The son of this peasant woman is going to die. Isn't that wonderful? He's at his last gasp. And all in line with our story—a husband from the other side of the mountain! And when you met him he was at the last gasp. So you're a widow. What do you say?

GRUSHA: It's true I could use a document with stamps on it for Michael.

LAVRENTI: Stamps make all the difference. Without something in writing the Shah couldn't prove he's a Shah. And you'll have a place to live.

GRUSHA: How much does the peasant woman want?

LAVRENTI: Four hundred piasters.

GRUSHA: Where will you find it?

LAVRENTI (*guiltily*): Aniko's milk money.

GRUSHA: No one would know us there. I'll do it.

LAVRENTI (*getting up*): I'll let the peasant woman know.
*Quick exit.*

GRUSHA: Michael, you make a lot of work. I came by you as the pear tree comes by sparrows. And because a Christian bends down and picks up a crust of bread so nothing will go to waste. Michael, it would have been better had I walked quickly away on that Easter Sunday in Nuka in the second courtyard. Now I *am* a fool.

SINGER:
The bridegroom was on his deathbed when the bride arrived. The bridegroom's mother was waiting at the door, telling her to hurry.

The bride brought a child along.
The witness hid it during the wedding.

*On one side the bed. Under the mosquito net lies a very sick man.* GRUSHA *is pulled in at a run by her future mother-in-law. They are followed by* LAVRENTI *and the* CHILD.

MOTHER-IN-LAW: Quick! Quick! Or he'll die on us before the wedding. *(To* LAVRENTI:*)* I was never told she had a child already.

LAVRENTI: What difference does it make? *(Pointing toward the dying man.)* It can't matter to him — in his condition.

MOTHER-IN-LAW: To him? But I'll never survive the shame! We are honest people. *(She begins to weep.)* My Jussup doesn't have to marry a girl with a child!

LAVRENTI: All right, make it another two hundred piasters. You'll have it in writing that the farm will go to you: but she'll have the right to live here for two years.

MOTHER-IN-LAW *(drying her tears)*: It'll hardly cover the funeral expenses. I hope she'll really lend a hand with the work. And what's happened to the monk? He must have slipped out through the kitchen window. We'll have the whole village on our necks when they hear Jussup's end is come! Oh dear! I'll go get the monk. But he mustn't see the child!

LAVRENTI: I'll take care he doesn't. But why only a monk? Why not a priest?

MOTHER-IN-LAW: Oh, he's just as good. I only made one mistake: I paid half his fee in advance. Enough to send him to the tavern. I only hope... *(She runs off.)*

LAVRENTI: She saved on the priest, the wretch! Hired a cheap monk.

GRUSHA: You *will* send Simon Shashava to see me if he turns up after all?

LAVRENTI: Yes. *(Pointing at the* SICK MAN.*)* Won't you take a look at him? *(*GRUSHA, *taking* MICHAEL *to her, shakes her head.)* He's not moving an eyelid. I hope we aren't too late.

*They listen. On the opposite side enter neighbors who look around and take up positions against the walls, thus forming another wall near the bed, yet leaving an opening so that the bed can be seen. They start murmuring prayers. Enter the* MOTHER-IN-LAW *with a* MONK. *Showing some annoyance and surprise, she bows to the guests.*

MOTHER-IN-LAW: I hope you won't mind waiting a few moments? My son's bride has just arrived from the city. An emergency wedding is about to be celebrated. *(To the* MONK *in the bedroom:)* I might have known you couldn't keep your trap shut. *(To* GRUSHA:*)* The wedding can take place at once. Here's the license. Me and the bride's brother *(*LAVRENTI *tries to hide in the background, after having quietly taken* MICHAEL *back from* GRUSHA. *The* MOTHER-IN-LAW *waves him away.)* are the witnesses.

GRUSHA *has bowed to the* MONK. *They go to the bed. The* MOTHER-IN-LAW *lifts the mosquito net. The* MONK *starts reeling off the marriage ceremony in Latin. Meanwhile the* MOTHER-IN-LAW *beckons to* LAVRENTI *to get rid of the* CHILD, *but fearing that it will cry he draws its attention to the ceremony,* GRUSHA *glances once at the* CHILD, *and* LAVRENTI *waves the* CHILD's *hand in a greeting.*

MONK: Are you prepared to be a faithful, obedient, and good wife to this man, and to cleave to him until death you do part?

GRUSHA *(looking at the* CHILD*)*: I am.

MONK *(to the* SICK PEASANT*)*: Are you prepared to be a good and loving husband to your wife until death you do part? *(As the* SICK PEASANT *does not answer, the* MONK *looks inquiringly around.)*

MOTHER-IN-LAW: Of course he is! Didn't you hear him say yes?

MONK: All right. We declare the marriage contracted! How about extreme unction?

MOTHER-IN-LAW: Nothing doing! The wedding cost quite enough. Now I must take care of the mourners. *(To* LAVRENTI:*)* Did we say seven hundred?

LAVRENTI: Six hundred. *(He pays.)* Now I don't want to sit with the guests and get to know people. So farewell, Grusha, and if my widowed sister comes to visit me, she'll get a welcome from my wife, or I'll show my teeth. *(Nods, gives the* CHILD *to* GRUSHA, *and leaves. The mourners glance after him without interest.)*

MONK: May one ask where this child comes from?

MOTHER-IN-LAW: Is there a child? I don't see a child. And you don't see a child either — you understand? Or it may turn out I saw all sorts of things in the tavern! Now come on.

*After* GRUSHA *has put the* CHILD *down and told him to be quiet, they move over left,* GRUSHA *is introduced to the neighbors.* This is my daughter-in-law. She arrived just in time to find dear Jussup still alive.

ONE WOMAN: He's been ill now a whole year, hasn't he? When our Vassili was drafted he was there to say good-bye.

ANOTHER WOMAN: Such things are terrible for a farm. The corn all ripe and the farmer in bed! It'll really be a blessing if he doesn't suffer too long, I say.

FIRST WOMAN *(confidentially)*: You know why we thought he'd taken to his bed? Because of the draft! And now his end is come!

MOTHER-IN-LAW: Sit yourselves down, please! And have some cakes!

*She beckons to* GRUSHA *and both women go into the bedroom, where they pick up the cake pans off the floor. The guests, among them the* MONK, *sit on the floor and begin conversing in subdued voices.*

ONE PEASANT *(to whom the* MONK *has handed the bottle which he has taken from his soutane)*: There's a child, you say! How can that have happened to Jussup?

A WOMAN: She was certainly lucky to get herself married, with him so sick!

MOTHER-IN-LAW: They're gossiping already. And wolfing down the funeral cakes at the same time! If he doesn't die today, I'll have to bake some more tomorrow!

GRUSHA: I'll bake them for you.

MOTHER-IN-LAW: Yesterday some horsemen rode by, and I went out to see who it was. When I came in again he was lying there like a corpse! So I sent for you. It can't take much longer. *(She listens.)*

MONK: Dear wedding and funeral guests! Deeply touched, we stand before a bed of death and marriage. The bride gets a veil; the groom, a shroud: how varied, my children, are the fates of men! Alas! One man dies and has a roof over his head, and the other is married and the flesh turns to dust from which it was made. Amen.

MOTHER-IN-LAW: He's getting his own back. I shouldn't have hired such a cheap one. It's what you'd expect. A more expensive monk would behave himself. In Sura there's one with a real air of sanctity about him, but of course he charges a fortune. A fifty piaster monk like that has no dignity, and as for piety, just fifty piasters' worth and no more! When I came to get him in the tavern he'd just made a speech, and he was shouting: "The war is over, beware of the peace!" We must go in.

GRUSHA *(giving* MICHAEL *a cake)*: Eat this cake, and keep nice and still, Michael.

*The two women offer cakes to the guests. The dying man sits up in bed. He puts his head out from under the mosquito net, stares at the two women, then sinks back again. The* MONK *takes two bottles from his soutane and offers them to the peasant beside him. Enter three* MUSICIANS *who are greeted with a sly wink by the* MONK.

MOTHER-IN-LAW *(to the* MUSICIANS*)*: What are you doing here? With instruments?

ONE MUSICIAN: Brother Anastasius here *(pointing at the* MONK*)* told us there was a wedding on.

MOTHER-IN-LAW: What? You brought them? Three more on my neck! Don't you know there's a dying man in the next room?

MONK: A very tempting assignment for a musician: something that could be either a subdued Wedding March or a spirited Funeral Dance.

MOTHER-IN-LAW: Well, you might as well play. Nobody can stop you eating in any case.

*The musicians play a potpourri. The women serve cakes.*

MONK: The trumpet sounds like a whining baby. And you, little drum, what have you got to tell the world?

DRUNKEN PEASANT *(beside the* MONK, *sings)*:
There was a young woman who said:
I thought I'd be happier, wed.
But my husband is old
And remarkably cold
So I sleep with a candle instead.

*The* MOTHER-IN-LAW *throws the* DRUNKEN PEASANT *out. The music stops. The guests are embarrassed.*

GUESTS *(loudly)*:

— Have you heard? The Grand Duke is back! But the Princes are against him.

— They say the Shah of Persia has lent him a great army to restore order in Grusinia.

— But how is that possible? The Shah of Persia is the enemy...

— The enemy of Grusinia, you donkey, not the enemy of the Grand Duke!

— In any case, the war's over, so our soldiers are coming back.

GRUSHA *drops a cake pan.* GUESTS *help her pick up the cake.*

AN OLD WOMAN *(to* GRUSHA*)*: Are you feeling bad? It's just excitement about dear Jussup. Sit down and rest a while, my dear. *(*GRUSHA *staggers.)*

GUESTS: Now everything'll be the way it was. Only the tax-es'll go up because now we'll have to pay for the war.

GRUSHA *(weakly)*: Did someone say the soldiers are back?

A MAN: I did.

GRUSHA: It can't be true.

FIRST MAN *(to a woman)*: Show her the shawl. We bought it from a soldier. It's from Persia.

GRUSHA *(looking at the shawl)*: They are here. *(She gets up, takes a step, kneels down in prayer, takes the silver cross and chain out of her blouse, and kisses it.)*

MOTHER-IN-LAW *(while the guests silently watch GRUSHA)*: What's the matter with you? Aren't you going to look after our guests? What's all this city nonsense got to do with us?

GUESTS *(resuming conversation while GRUSHA remains in prayer)*:
—You can buy Persian saddles from the soldiers too. Though many want crutches in exchange for them.
—The leaders on one side can win a war, the soldiers on both sides lose it.
—Anyway, the war's over. It's something they can't draft you any more.

*The dying man sits bolt upright in bed. He listens.*

—What we need is two weeks of good weather.
—Our pear trees are hardly bearing a thing this year.

MOTHER-IN-LAW *(offering cakes)*: Have some more cakes and welcome! There are more!

*The* MOTHER-IN-LAW *goes to the bedroom with the empty cake pans. Unaware of the dying man, she is bending down to pick up another tray when he begins to talk in a hoarse voice.*

PEASANT: How many more cakes are you going to stuff down their throats? D'you think I can shit money?

*The* MOTHER-IN-LAW *starts, stares at him aghast, while he climbs out from behind the mosquito net.*

FIRST WOMAN *(talking kindly to GRUSHA in the next room)*: Has the young wife got someone at the front?

A MAN: It's good news that they're on their way home, huh?

PEASANT: Don't stare at me like that! Where's this wife you've saddled me with?

*Receiving no answer, he climbs out of bed and in his nightshirt staggers into the other room. Trembling, she follows him with the cake pan.*

GUESTS *(seeing him and shrieking)*: Good God! Jussup!

*Everyone leaps up in alarm. The women rush to the door.* GRUSHA, *still on her knees, turns round and stares at the man.*

PEASANT: A funeral supper! You'd enjoy that, wouldn't you? Get out before I throw you out! *(As the guests stampede from the house, gloomily to* GRUSHA:*)* I've upset the apple cart, huh? *(Receiving no answer, he turns round and takes a cake from the pan which his mother is holding.)*

SINGER:

O confusion! The wife discovers she has a husband.

By day there's the child, by night there's the husband.

The lover is on his way both day and night.

Husband and wife look at each other.

The bedroom is small.

*Near the bed the* PEASANT *is sitting in a high wooden bathtub, naked, the* MOTHER-IN-LAW *is pouring water from a pitcher. Opposite* GRUSHA *cowers with* MICHAEL, *who is playing at mending straw mats.*

PEASANT *(to his mother)*: That's her work, not yours. Where's she hiding out now?

MOTHER-IN-LAW *(calling)*: Grusha! The peasant wants you!

GRUSHA *(to* MICHAEL*)*: There are still two holes to mend.

PEASANT *(when* GRUSHA *approaches)*: Scrub my back!

GRUSHA: Can't the peasant do it himself?

PEASANT: "Can't the peasant do it himself?" Get the brush! To hell with you! Are you the wife here? Or are you a visitor? *(To the* MOTHER-IN-LAW:*)* It's too cold!

MOTHER-IN-LAW: I'll run for hot water.

GRUSHA: Let me go.

PEASANT: You stay here. *(The* MOTHER-IN-LAW *exits.)* Rub harder. And no shirking. You've seen a naked fellow before. That child didn't come out of thin air.

GRUSHA: The child was not conceived in joy, if that's what the peasant means.

PEASANT *(turning and grinning)*: You don't look the type. *(*GRUSHA *stops scrubbing him, starts back. Enter the* MOTHER-IN-LAW.*)*

PEASANT: A nice thing you've saddled me with! A simpleton for a wife!

MOTHER-IN-LAW: She just isn't cooperative.

PEASANT: Pour—but go easy! Ow! Go easy, I said. *(To* GRUSHA:*)* Maybe you did something wrong in the city... I wouldn't be surprised. Why else should you be here? But I won't talk about that. I've not said a word about the illegitimate object you brought into my house either. But my patience has limits! It's against nature. *(To the* MOTHER-IN-LAW:*)* More! *(To* GRUSHA:*)* And even if your soldier does come back, you're married.

GRUSHA: Yes.

PEASANT: But your soldier won't come back. Don't you believe it.

GRUSHA: No.

PEASANT: You're cheating me. You're my wife and you're not my wife. Where you lie, nothing lies, and yet no other woman can lie there. When I go to work in the morning I'm tired— when I lie down at night I'm awake as the devil. God has given you sex—and what d'you do? I don't have ten piasters to buy myself a woman in the city. Besides, it's a long way. Woman weeds the fields and opens up her legs, that's what our calendar says. D'you hear?

GRUSHA *(quietly)*: Yes. I didn't mean to cheat you out of it.

PEASANT: She didn't mean to cheat me out of it! Pour some more water! *(The* MOTHER-IN-LAW *pours.)* Ow!

SINGER:

> As she sat by the stream to wash the linen
> She saw his image in the water
> And his face grew dimmer with the passing moons.
> As she raised herself to wring the linen
> She heard his voice from the murmuring maple
> And his voice grew fainter with the passing moons.
> Evasions and sighs grew more numerous,
> Tears and sweat flowed.
> With the passing moons the child grew up.

GRUSHA *sits by a stream, dipping linen into the water. In the rear, a few children are standing.*

GRUSHA *(to* MICHAEL*)*: You can play with them, Michael, but don't let them boss you around just because you're the littlest. *(*MICHAEL *nods and joins the children. They start playing.)*

BIGGEST BOY: Today it's the Heads-Off Game. *(To a* FAT BOY:*)* You're the Prince and you laugh. *(To* MICHAEL:*)* You're the Governor. *(To a* GIRL:*)* You're the Governor's wife and you cry when his head's cut off. And I do the cutting. *(He shows his wooden sword.)* With this. First, they lead the Governor into the yard. The Prince walks in front. The Governor's wife comes last.

*They form a procession. The* FAT BOY *is first and laughs. Then comes* MICHAEL, *then the* BIGGEST BOY, *and then the* GIRL, *who weeps.*

MICHAEL *(standing still)*: Me cut off head!

BIGGEST BOY: That's my job. You're the littlest. The Governor's the easy part. All you do is kneel down and get your head cut off — simple.

MICHAEL: Me want sword!

BIGGEST BOY: It's mine! *(He gives* MICHAEL *a kick.)*

GIRL *(shouting to* GRUSHA*)*: He won't play his part!

GRUSHA *(laughing)*: Even the little duck is a swimmer, they say.

BIGGEST BOY: You can be the Prince if you can laugh. (MICHAEL *shakes his head.*)

FAT BOY: I laugh best. Let him cut off the head just once. Then you do it, then me.

*Reluctantly, the* BIGGEST BOY *hands* MICHAEL *the wooden sword and kneels down. The* FAT BOY *sits down, slaps his thigh, and laughs with all his might. The* GIRL *weeps loudly.* MICHAEL *swings the big sword and "cuts off" the head. In doing so, he topples over.*

BIGGEST BOY: Hey! I'll show you how to cut heads off!

MICHAEL *runs away. The children run after him.* GRUSHA *laughs, following them with her eyes. On looking back, she sees* SIMON SHASHAVA *standing on the opposite bank. He wears a shabby uniform.*

GRUSHA: Simon!

SIMON: Is that Grusha Vashnadze?

GRUSHA: Simon!

SIMON *(formally)*: A good morning to the young lady. I hope she is well.

GRUSHA *(getting up gaily and bowing low)*: A good morning to the soldier. God be thanked he has returned in good health.

SIMON: They found better fish, so they didn't eat me, said the haddock.

GRUSHA: Courage, said the kitchen boy. Good luck, said the hero.

SIMON: How are things here? Was the winter bearable? The neighbor considerate?

GRUSHA: The winter was a trifle rough, the neighbor as usual, Simon.

SIMON: May one ask if a certain person still dips her toes in the water when rinsing the linen?

GRUSHA: The answer is no. Because of the eyes in the bushes.

SIMON: The young lady is speaking of soldiers. Here stands a paymaster.

GRUSHA: A job worth twenty piasters?

SIMON: And lodgings.

GRUSHA *(with tears in her eyes)*: Behind the barracks under the date trees.

SIMON: Yes, there. A certain person has kept her eyes open.

GRUSHA: She has, Simon.

SIMON: And has not forgotten? *(GRUSHA shakes her head.)* So the door is still on its hinges as they say? *(GRUSHA looks at him in silence and shakes her head again.)* What's this? Is anything not as it should be?

GRUSHA: Simon Shashava, I can never return to Nuka. Something has happened.

SIMON: What can have happened?

GRUSHA: For one thing, I knocked an Ironshirt down.

SIMON: Grusha Vashnadze must have had her reasons for that.

GRUSHA: Simon Shashava, I am no longer called what I used to be called.

SIMON *(after a pause)*: I do not understand.

GRUSHA: When do women change their names, Simon? Let me explain. Nothing stands between us. Everything is just as it was. You must believe that.

SIMON: Nothing stands between us and yet there's something?

GRUSHA: How can I explain it so fast and with the stream between us? Couldn't you cross the bridge there?

SIMON: Maybe it's no longer necessary.

GRUSHA: It is very necessary. Come over on this side, Simon. Quick!

SIMON: Does the young lady wish to say someone has come too late?

GRUSHA *looks up at him in despair, her face streaming with tears.* SIMON *stares before him. He picks up a piece of wood and starts cutting it.*

SINGER:

So many words are said, so many left unsaid.

The soldier has come.

Where he comes from, he does not say.

Hear what he thought and did not say:
"The battle began, gray at dawn, grew bloody at noon.
The first man fell in front of me, the second behind me, the
    third at my side.
I trod on the first, left the second behind, the third was run
    through by the captain.
One of my brothers died by steel, the other by smoke.
My neck caught fire, my hands froze in my gloves, my toes
    in my socks.
I fed on aspen buds, I drank maple juice, I slept on stone, in
    water."

SIMON: I see a cap in the grass. Is there a little one already?

GRUSHA: There is, Simon. There's no keeping *that* from you.
But please don't worry, it is not mine.

SIMON: When the wind once starts to blow, they say, it blows
through every cranny. The wife need say no more. (GRUSHA
*looks into her lap and is silent.)*

SINGER:
There was yearning but there was no waiting.
The oath is broken. Neither could say why.
Hear what she thought but did not say:
"While you fought in the battle, soldier,
The bloody battle, the bitter battle
I found a helpless infant
I had not the heart to destroy him
I had to care for a creature that was lost
I had to stoop for breadcrumbs on the floor
I had to break myself for that which was not mine
That which was other people's.
Someone must help!
For the little tree needs water
The lamb loses its way when the shepherd is asleep
And its cry is unheard!"

SIMON: Give me back the cross I gave you. Better still, throw
it in the stream. *(He turns to go.)*

GRUSHA *(getting up)*: Simon Shashava, don't go away! He isn't mine! He isn't mine! *(She hears the children calling.)* What's the matter, children?

VOICES: Soldiers! And they're taking Michael away!

GRUSHA *stands aghast as two* IRONSHIRTS, *with* MICHAEL *between them, come toward her.*

ONE OF THE IRONSHIRTS: Are you Grusha? *(She nods.)* Is this your child?

GRUSHA: Yes. *(SIMON goes.)* Simon!

IRONSHIRT: We have orders, in the name of the law, to take this child, found in your custody, back to the city. It is suspected that the child is Michael Abashwili, son and heir of the late Governor Georgi Abashwili, and his wife, Natella Abashwili. Here is the document and the seal. *(They lead the CHILD away.)*

GRUSHA *(running after them, shouting)*: Leave him here. Please! He's mine!

SINGER:

The Ironshirts took the child, the beloved child.

The unhappy girl followed them to the city, the dreaded city.

She who had borne him demanded the child.

She who had raised him faced trial.

Who will decide the case?

To whom will the child be assigned?

Who will the judge be? A good judge? A bad?

The city was in flames.

In the judge's seat sat Azdak.[1]

---

1. The name Azdak should be accented on the second syllable.

# 4

# The Story of the Judge

SINGER:

Hear the story of the judge

How he turned judge, how he passed judgment, what kind of judge he was.

On that Easter Sunday of the great revolt, when the Grand Duke was overthrown

And his Governor Abashwili, father of our child, lost his head

The Village Scrivener Azdak found a fugitive in the woods and hid him in his hut.

AZDAK, *in rags and slightly drunk, is helping an old beggar into his cottage.*

AZDAK: Stop snorting, you're not a horse. And it won't do you any good with the police to run like a snotty nose in April. Stand still, I say. *(He catches the* OLD MAN, *who has marched into the cottage as if he'd like to go through the walls.)* Sit down. Feed. Here's a hunk of cheese. *(From under some rags, in a chest, he fishes out some cheese, and the* OLD MAN *greedily begins to eat.)* Haven't eaten in a long time, huh? *(The* OLD MAN *growls.)* Why were you running like that, asshole? The cop wouldn't even have seen you.

OLD MAN: Had to! Had to!

AZDAK: Blue funk? *(The* OLD MAN *stares, uncomprehending.)* Cold feet? Panic? Don't lick your chops like a Grand Duke. Or an old sow. I can't stand it. We have to accept respectable stinkers as God made them, but not you! I once heard of a senior judge who farted at a public dinner to show an independent spirit! Watching you eat like that gives me the most awful ideas. Why don't you say something? *(Sharply.)* Show me your hand. Can't you hear? *(The* OLD MAN *slowly puts out his hand.)* White! So you're not a beggar at all! A fraud, a walking swindle! And I'm hiding you from the cops like you were an honest man! Why were you running like that if you're a landowner? For that's what you are. Don't deny it! I see it in your guilty face! *(He gets up.)* Get out! *(The* OLD MAN *looks at him uncertainly.)* What are you waiting for, peasant-flogger?

OLD MAN: Pursued. Need undivided attention. Make proposition . . .·

AZDAK: Make what? A proposition? Well, if that isn't the height of insolence. He's making me a proposition! The bitten man scratches his fingers bloody, and the leech that's biting him makes him a proposition! Get out, I tell you!

OLD MAN: Understand point of view! Persuasion! Pay hundred thousand piasters one night! Yes?

AZDAK: What, you think you can buy me? For a hundred thousand piasters? Let's say a hundred and fifty thousand. Where are they?

OLD MAN: Have not them here. Of course. Will be sent. Hope do not doubt.

AZDAK: Doubt very much. Get out!

*The* OLD MAN *gets up, waddles to the door. A* VOICE *is heard offstage.*

VOICE: Azdak!

*The* OLD MAN *turns, waddles to the opposite corner, stands still.*

AZDAK *(calling out)*: I'm not in! *(He walks to door.)* So you're sniffing around here again, Shauwa?

SHAUWA *(reproachfully)*: You caught another rabbit, Azdak. And you'd promised me it wouldn't happen again!

AZDAK *(severely)*: Shauwa, don't talk about things you don't understand. The rabbit is a dangerous and destructive beast. It feeds on plants, especially on the species of plants known as weeds. It must therefore be exterminated.

SHAUWA: Azdak, don't be so hard on me. I'll lose my job if I don't arrest you. I know you have a good heart.

AZDAK: I do not have a good heart! How often must I tell you I'm a man of intellect?

SHAUWA *(slyly)*: I know, Azdak. You're a superior person. You say so yourself. I'm just a Christian and an ignoramus. So I ask you: When one of the Prince's rabbits is stolen, and I'm a policeman, what should I do with the offending party?

AZDAK: Shauwa, Shauwa, shame on you. You stand and ask me a question, than which nothing could be more seductive. It's like you were a woman — let's say that bad girl Nunowna, and you showed me your thigh — Nunowna's thigh, that would be — and asked me: "What shall I do with my thigh, it itches?" Is she as innocent as she pretends? Of course not. I catch a rabbit, but you catch a man. Man is made in God's image. Not so a rabbit, you know that. I'm a rabbit-eater, but you're a man-eater, Shauwa. And God will pass judgment on you. Shauwa, go home and repent. No, stop, there's something... *(He looks at the* OLD MAN *who stands trembling in the corner.)* No, it's nothing. Go home and repent. *(He slams the door behind* SHAUWA.*)* Now you're surprised, huh? Surprised I didn't hand you over? I couldn't hand over a bedbug to that animal. It goes against the grain. Now don't tremble because of a cop! So old and still so scared? Finish your cheese, but eat it like a poor man, or else they'll still catch you. Must I even explain how a poor man behaves? *(He pushes him down, and then gives him back the cheese.)* That box is the table.

Lay your elbows on the table. Now, encircle the cheese on the plate like it might be snatched from you at any moment—what right have you to be safe, huh?—now, hold your knife like an undersized sickle, and give your cheese a troubled look because, like all beautiful things, it's already fading away. *(AZDAK watches him.)* They're after you, which speaks in your favor, but how can we be sure they're not mistaken about you? In Tiflis one time they hanged a landowner, a Turk, who could prove he quartered his peasants instead of merely cutting them in half, as is the custom, and he squeezed twice the usual amount of taxes out of them, his zeal was above suspicion. And yet they hanged him like a common criminal—because he was a Turk—a thing he couldn't do much about. What injustice! He got onto the gallows by a sheer fluke. In short, I don't trust you.

SINGER:
Thus Azdak gave the old beggar a bed,
And learned that old beggar was the old butcher, the Grand Duke himself,
And was ashamed.
He denounced himself and ordered the policeman to take him to Nuka, to court, to be judged.

*In the court of justice three* IRONSHIRTS *sit drinking. From a beam hangs a man in judge's robes. Enter* AZDAK, *in chains, dragging* SHAUWA *behind him.*

AZDAK *(shouting)*: I've helped the Grand Duke, the Grand Thief, the Grand Butcher, to escape! In the name of justice I ask to be severely judged in public trial!

FIRST IRONSHIRT: Who's this queer bird?

SHAUWA: That's our Village Scrivener, Azdak.

AZDAK: I am contemptible! I am a traitor! A branded criminal! Tell them, flatfoot, how I insisted on being tied up and brought to the capital. Because I sheltered the Grand Duke, the Grand Swindler, by mistake. And how I found out afterwards. See the marked man denounce himself! Tell them how I forced you to walk half the night with me to clear the whole thing up.

SHAUWA: And all by threats. That wasn't nice of you, Azdak.

AZDAK: Shut your mouth, Shauwa. You don't understand. A new age is upon us! It'll go thundering over you. You're finished. The police will be wiped out — poof! Everything will be gone into, everything will be brought into the open. The guilty will give themselves up. Why? They couldn't escape the people in any case. *(To* SHAUWA:*)* Tell them how I shouted all along Shoemaker Street *(with big gestures, looking at the* IRONSHIRTS*)* "In my ignorance I let the Grand Swindler escape! So tear me to pieces, brothers!" I wanted to get it in first.

FIRST IRONSHIRT: And what did your brothers answer?

SHAUWA: They comforted him in Butcher Street, and they laughed themselves sick in Shoemaker Street. That's all.

AZDAK: But with you it's different. I can see you're men of iron. Brothers, where's the judge? I must be tried.

FIRST IRONSHIRT *(pointing at the hanged man)*: There's the judge. And please stop "brothering" us. It's rather a sore spot this evening.

AZDAK: "There's the judge." An answer never heard in Grusinia before. Townsman, where's His Excellency the Governor? *(Pointing to the ground.)* There's His Excellency, stranger. Where's the Chief Tax Collector? Where's the official Recruiting Officer? The Patriarch? The Chief of Police? There, there, there — all there. Brothers, I expected no less of you.

SECOND IRONSHIRT: What? *What* was it you expected, funny man?

AZDAK: What happened in Persia, brother, what happened in Persia?

SECOND IRONSHIRT: What did happen in Persia?

AZDAK: Everybody was hanged. Viziers, tax collectors. Everybody. Forty years ago now. My grandfather, a remarkable man by the way, saw it all. For three whole days. Everywhere.

SECOND IRONSHIRT: And who ruled when the Vizier was hanged?

AZDAK: A peasant ruled when the Vizier was hanged.

SECOND IRONSHIRT: And who commanded the army?

AZDAK: A soldier, soldier.

SECOND IRONSHIRT: And who paid the wages?

AZDAK: A dyer. A dyer paid the wages.

SECOND IRONSHIRT: Wasn't it a weaver, maybe?

FIRST IRONSHIRT: And why did all this happen, Persian?

AZDAK: Why did all this happen? Must there be a special reason? Why do you scratch yourself, brother? War! Too long a war! And no justice! My grandfather brought back a song that tells how it was. I will sing it for you. With my friend the policeman. *(To* SHAUWA:*)* And hold the rope tight. It's very suitable. *(He sings, with* SHAUWA *holding the rope tight around him.)*


THE SONG OF INJUSTICE IN PERSIA

Why don't our sons bleed any more? Why don't our daughters weep?

Why do only the slaughterhouse cattle have blood in their veins?

Why do only the willows shed tears on Lake Urmia?

The king must have a new province, the peasant must give up his savings.

That the roof of the world might be conquered, the roof of the cottage is torn down.

Our men are carried to the ends of the earth, so that great ones can eat at home.

The soldiers kill each other, the marshals salute each other.

They bite the widow's tax money to see if it's good, their swords break.

The battle was lost, the helmets were paid for.

*Refrain:* Is it so? Is it so?

SHAUWA *(refrain)*: Yes, yes, yes, yes, yes it's so.

AZDAK: Want to hear the rest of it? *(The* FIRST IRONSHIRT *nods.)*

SECOND IRONSHIRT *(to* SHAUWA*)*: Did he teach you that song?

SHAUWA: Yes, only my voice isn't very good.

SECOND IRONSHIRT: No. *(To* AZDAK:*)* Go on singing.

AZDAK: The second verse is about the peace. *(He sings.)*

The offices are packed, the streets overflow with officials.
The rivers jump their banks and ravage the fields.
Those who cannot let down their own trousers rule countries.
They can't count up to four, but they devour eight courses.
The corn farmers, looking round for buyers, see only the starving.
The weavers go home from their looms in rags.
*Refrain*: Is it so? Is it so?

SHAUWA *(refrain)*: Yes, yes, yes, yes, yes it's so.

AZDAK:

That's why our sons don't bleed any more, that's why our daughters don't weep.

That's why only the slaughterhouse cattle have blood in their veins,

And only the willows shed tears by Lake Urmia toward morning.

FIRST IRONSHIRT: Are you going to sing that song here in town?

AZDAK: Sure. What's wrong with it?

FIRST IRONSHIRT: Have you noticed that the sky's getting red? *(Turning round,* AZDAK *sees the sky red with fire.)* It's the people's quarters on the outskirts of town. The carpet weavers have caught the "Persian Sickness," too. And they've been asking if Prince Kazbeki isn't eating too many courses. This morning they strung up the city judge. As for us we beat them to pulp. We were paid one hundred piasters per man, you understand?

AZDAK (*after a pause*): I understand. (*He glances shyly round and, creeping away, sits down in a corner, his head in his hands.*)

IRONSHIRTS (*to each other*): If there ever was a troublemaker it's him.

—He must've come to the capital to fish in the troubled waters.

SHAUWA: Oh, I don't think he's a really bad character, gentlemen. Steals a few chickens here and there. And maybe a rabbit.

SECOND IRONSHIRT (*approaching* AZDAK): Came to fish in the troubled waters, huh?

AZDAK (*looking up*): I don't know why I came.

SECOND IRONSHIRT: Are you in with the carpet weavers maybe? (AZDAK *shakes his head.*) How about that song?

AZDAK: From my grandfather. A silly and ignorant man.

SECOND IRONSHIRT: Right. And how about the dyer who paid the wages?

AZDAK (*muttering*): That was in Persia.

FIRST IRONSHIRT: And this denouncing of yourself? Because you didn't hang the Grand Duke with your own hands?

AZDAK: Didn't I tell you I let him run? (*He creeps farther away and sits on the floor.*)

SHAUWA: I can swear to that: he let him run.

*The* IRONSHIRTS *burst out laughing and slap* SHAUWA *on the back.* AZDAK *laughs loudest. They slap* AZDAK *too, and unchain him. They all start drinking as the* FAT PRINCE *enters with a young man.*

FIRST IRONSHIRT (*to* AZDAK, *pointing at the* FAT PRINCE): There's your "new age" for you! (*More laughter.*)

FAT PRINCE: Well, my friends, what is there to laugh about? Permit me a serious word. Yesterday morning the Princes of Grusinia overthrew the warmongering government of the Grand Duke and did away with his Governors. Unfortunately the Grand Duke himself escaped. In this fateful hour our carpet weavers, those eternal troublemakers, had the effrontery to stir up a rebellion and hang the universally loved city judge, our dear Illo Orbeliani. Ts — ts — ts. My friends, we need peace, peace, peace in Grusinia! And justice! So I've brought along my dear nephew Bizergan Kazbeki. He'll be the new judge, hm? A very gifted fellow. What do you say? I want your opinion. Let the people decide!

SECOND IRONSHIRT: Does this mean *we* elect the judge?

FAT PRINCE: Precisely. Let the people propose some very gifted fellow! Confer among yourselves, my friends. *(The* IRONSHIRTS *confer.)* Don't worry, my little fox. The job's yours. And when we catch the Grand Duke we won't have to kiss this rabble's ass any longer.

IRONSHIRTS *(among themselves)*:
—Very funny: they're wetting their pants because they haven't caught the Grand Duke.
—When the outlook isn't so bright, they say: "My friends!" and "Let the people decide!"
—Now he even wants justice for Grusinia! But fun is fun as long as it lasts! *(Pointing at* AZDAK.*) He* knows all about justice. Hey, rascal, would you like this nephew fellow to be the judge?

AZDAK: Are you asking me? You're not asking *me?!*

FIRST IRONSHIRT: Why not? Anything for a laugh!

AZDAK: You'd like to test him to the marrow, correct? Have you a criminal on hand? An experienced one? So the candidate can show what he knows?

SECOND IRONSHIRT: Let's see. We do have a couple of doctors downstairs. Let's use them.

AZDAK: Oh, no, that's no good, we can't take real criminals till we're sure the judge will be appointed. He may be dumb, but he must be appointed, or the law is violated. And the law is a sensitive organ. It's like the spleen, you mustn't hit it — that would be fatal. Of course you can hang those two without violating the law, because there was no judge in the vicinity. But judgment, when pronounced, must be pronounced with absolute gravity — it's all such nonsense. Suppose, for instance, a judge jails a woman—let's say she's stolen a corn cake to feed her child—and this judge isn't wearing his robes—or maybe he's scratching himself while passing sentence and half his body is uncovered—a man's thigh *will* itch once in a while—the sentence this judge passes is a disgrace and the law is violated. In short it would be easier for a judge's robe and a judge's hat to pass judgment than for a man with no robe and no hat. If you don't treat it with respect, the law just disappears on you. Now you don't try out a bottle of wine by offering it to a dog; you'd only lose your wine.

FIRST IRONSHIRT: Then what do you suggest, hairsplitter?

AZDAK: I'll be the defendant.

FIRST IRONSHIRT: You? *(He bursts out laughing.)*

FAT PRINCE: What have you decided?

FIRST IRONSHIRT: We've decided to stage a rehearsal. Our friend here will be the defendant. Let the candidate be the judge and sit there.

FAT PRINCE: It isn't customary, but why not? *(To the* NEPHEW:*)* A mere formality, my little fox. What have I taught you? Who got there first—the slow runner or the fast?

NEPHEW: The silent runner, Uncle Arsen.

*The* NEPHEW *takes the chair. The* IRONSHIRTS *and the* FAT PRINCE *sit on the steps. Enter* AZDAK, *mimicking the gait of the Grand Duke.*

AZDAK *(in the Grand Duke's accent)*: Is any here knows me? Am Grand Duke.

IRONSHIRTS:

— *What* is he?

— The Grand Duke. He knows him, too.

— Fine. So get on with the trial.

AZDAK: Listen! Am accused instigating war? Ridiculous! Am saying ridiculous! That enough? If not, have brought lawyers. Believe five hundred. *(He points behind him, pretending to be surrounded by lawyers.)* Requisition all available seats for lawyers! *(The* IRONSHIRTS *laugh; the* FAT PRINCE *joins in.)*

NEPHEW *(to the* IRONSHIRTS*)*: You really wish me to try this case? I find it rather unusual. From the taste angle, I mean.

FIRST IRONSHIRT: Let's go!

FAT PRINCE *(smiling)*: Let him have it, my little fox!

NEPHEW: All right. People of Grusinia versus Grand Duke. Defendant, what have you got to say for yourself?

AZDAK: Plenty. Naturally, have read war lost. Only started on the advice of patriots. Like Uncle Arsen Kazbeki. Call Uncle Arsen as witness.

FAT PRINCE *(to the* IRONSHIRTS, *delightedly)*: What a madcap!

NEPHEW: Motion rejected. One cannot be arraigned for declaring a war, which every ruler has to do once in a while, but only for running a war badly.

AZDAK: Rubbish! Did not run it at all! Had it run! Had it run by Princes! Naturally, they messed it up.

NEPHEW: Do you by any chance deny having been commander-in-chief?

AZDAK: Not at all! Always *was* commander-in-chief. At birth shouted at wet nurse. Was trained drop turds in toilet, grew accustomed to command. Always commanded officials rob my cash box. Officers flog soldiers only on command. Landowners sleep with peasants' wives only on strictest command. Uncle Arsen here grew his belly at *my* command!

IRONSHIRTS *(clapping)*: He's good! Long live the Grand Duke!

FAT PRINCE: Answer him, my little fox: I'm with you.

NEPHEW: I shall answer him according to the dignity of the law. Defendant, preserve the dignity of the law!

AZDAK: Agreed. Command you proceed with trial!

NEPHEW: It is not your place to command me. You claim that the Princes forced you to declare war. How can you claim, then, that they — er — "messed it up"?

AZDAK: Did not send enough people. Embezzled funds. Sent sick horses. During attack, drinking in whorehouse. Call Uncle Arsen as witness.

NEPHEW: Are you making the outrageous suggestion that the Princes of this country did not fight?

AZDAK: No. Princes fought. Fought for war contracts.

FAT PRINCE *(jumping up)*: That's too much! This man talks like a carpet weaver!

AZDAK: Really? Told nothing but truth.

FAT PRINCE: Hang him! Hang him!

FIRST IRONSHIRT *(pulling the* PRINCE *down)*: Keep quiet! Go on, Excellency!

NEPHEW: Quiet! I now render a verdict: You must be hanged! By the neck! Having lost war!

AZDAK: Young man, seriously advise not fall publicly into jerky clipped speech. Cannot be watchdog if howl like wolf. Got it? If people realize Princes speak same language as Grand Duke, may hang Grand Duke *and Princes,* huh? By the way, must overrule verdict. Reason? War lost, but not for Princes. Princes won their war. Got 3,863,000 piasters for horses not delivered, 8,240,000 piasters for food supplies not produced. Are therefore victors. War lost only for Grusinia, which is not present in this court.

FAT PRINCE: I think that will do, my friends. *(To* AZDAK:*)* You can withdraw, funny man. *(To the* IRONSHIRTS:*)* You may now ratify the new judge's appointment, my friends.

FIRST IRONSHIRT: Yes, we can. Take down the judge's gown. *(One* IRONSHIRT *climbs on the back of the other, pulls the gown off the hanged man.)* *(To the* NEPHEW:*)* Now you run away so the right ass can get on the right chair. *(To* AZDAK:*)* Step forward! Go to the judge's seat! Now sit in it! *(*AZDAK *steps up, bows, and sits down.)* The judge was always a rascal! Now the rascal shall be a judge! *(The judge's gown is placed round his shoulders, the hat on his head.)* And what a judge!

SINGER:

And there was civil war in the land.

The mighty were not safe.

And Azdak was made a judge by the Ironshirts.

And Azdak remained a judge for two years.

SINGER AND CHORUS:

When the towns were set afire

And rivers of blood rose higher and higher,

Cockroaches crawled out of every crack.

And the court was full of schemers

And the church of foul blasphemers.

In the judge's cassock sat Azdak.

AZDAK *sits in the judge's chair, peeling an apple.* SHAUWA *is sweeping out the hall. On one side an* INVALID *in a wheelchair. Opposite, a young man accused of blackmail. An* IRONSHIRT *stands guard, holding the Ironshirts' banner.*

AZDAK: In consideration of the large number of cases, the Court today will hear two cases at a time. Before I open the proceedings, a short announcement — I accept. *(He stretches out his hand. The* BLACKMAILER *is the only one to produce any money. He hands it to* AZDAK.*)* I reserve the right to punish one of the parties for contempt of court. *(He glances at the* INVALID.*)* You *(to the* DOCTOR*)* are a doctor, and you *(to the* INVALID*)* are bringing a complaint against him. Is the doctor responsible for your condition?

INVALID: Yes. I had a stroke on his account.

AZDAK: That would be professional negligence.

INVALID: Worse than negligence. I gave this man money for his studies. So far, he hasn't paid me back a cent. It was when I heard he was treating a patient free that I had my stroke.

AZDAK: Rightly. *(To a* LIMPING MAN:*)* And what are *you* doing here?

LIMPING MAN: I'm the patient, Your Honor.

AZDAK: He treated your leg for nothing?

LIMPING MAN: The wrong leg! My rheumatism was in the left leg, he operated on the right. That's why I limp.

AZDAK: And you were treated free?

INVALID: A five-hundred-piaster operation free! For nothing! For a God-bless-you! And I paid for this man's studies! *(To the* DOCTOR:*)* Did they teach you to operate free?

DOCTOR: Your Honor, it is the custom to demand the fee before the operation, as the patient is more willing to pay before an operation than after. Which is only human. In the case in question I was convinced, when I started the operation, that my servant had already received the fee. In this I was mistaken.

INVALID: He was mistaken! A good doctor doesn't make mistakes! He examines before he operates!

AZDAK: That's right: *(To* SHAUWA:*)* Public Prosecutor, what's the other case about?

SHAUWA *(busily sweeping)*: Blackmail.

BLACKMAILER: High Court of Justice, I'm innocent. I only wanted to find out from the landowner concerned if he really *had* raped his niece. He informed me very politely that this was not the case, and gave me the money only so I could pay for my uncle's studies.

AZDAK: Hm. *(To the* DOCTOR:*)* You, on the other hand, can cite no extenuating circumstances for your offense, huh?

DOCTOR: Except that to err is human.

AZDAK: And you are aware that in money matters a good doctor is a highly responsible person? I once heard of a doctor who got a thousand piasters for a sprained finger by remarking that sprains have something to do with blood circulation, which after all a less good doctor might have overlooked, and who, on another occasion made a real gold mine out of a somewhat disordered gall bladder, he treated it with such loving care. You have no excuse, Doctor. The corn merchant Uxu had his son study medicine to get some knowledge of trade, our medical schools are so good. *(To the* BLACKMAIL-ER:*)* What's the landowner's name?

SHAUWA: He doesn't want it mentioned.

AZDAK: In that case I will pass judgement. The Court considers the blackmail proved. And you *(to the* INVALID*)* are sentenced to a fine of one thousand piasters. If you have a second stroke, the doctor will have to treat you free. Even if he has to amputate. *(To the* LIMPING MAN:*)* As compensation, you will receive a bottle of rubbing alcohol. *(To the* BLACK-MAILER:*)* You are sentenced to hand over half the proceeds of your deal to the Public Prosecutor to keep the landowner's name secret. You are advised, moreover, to study medicine — you seem well suited to that calling. *(To the* DOCTOR:*)* You have perpetrated an unpardonable error in the practice of your profession: you are acquitted. Next cases!

SINGER AND CHORUS:
Men won't do much for a shilling.
For a pound they may be willing.
For twenty pounds the verdict's in the sack.
As for the many, all too many,
Those who've only got a penny —
They've one single, sole recourse: Azdak.

*Enter* AZDAK *from the caravansary on the highroad, followed by an old bearded* INNKEEPER. *The judge's chair is carried by a stableman and* SHAUWA. *An* IRONSHIRT, *with a banner, takes up his position.*

AZDAK: Put me down. Then we'll get some air, maybe even a good stiff breeze from the lemon grove there. It does justice good to be done in the open: the wind blows her skirts up and you can see what she's got. Shauwa, we've been eating too much. These official journeys are exhausting. *(To the* INN-KEEPER:*)* It's a question of your daughter-in-law?

INNKEEPER: Your Worship, it's a question of the family honor. I wish to bring an action on behalf of my son, who's away

on business on the other side the mountain. This is the offending stableman, and here's my daughter-in-law.
*Enter the* DAUGHTER-IN-LAW, *a voluptuous wench. She is veiled.*

AZDAK *(sitting down)*: I accept. *(Sighing, the* INNKEEPER *hands him some money.)* Good. Now the formalities are disposed of. This is a case of rape?

INNKEEPER: Your Honor, I caught the fellow in the act. Ludovica was in the straw on the stable floor.

AZDAK: Quite right, the stable. Lovely horses! I specially liked the little roan.

INNKEEPER: The first thing I did, of course, was to question Ludovica. On my son's behalf.

AZDAK *(seriously)*: I said I specially liked the little roan.

INNKEEPER *(coldly)*: Really? Ludovica confessed the stableman took her against her will.

AZDAK: Take your veil off, Ludovica. *(She does so.)* Ludovica, you please the Court. Tell us how it happened.

LUDOVICA *(well schooled)*: When I entered the stable to see the new foal the stableman said to me on his own accord: "It's hot today!" and laid his hand on my left breast. I said to him: "Don't do that!" But he continued to handle me indecently, which provoked my anger. Before I realized his sinful intentions, he got much closer. It was all over when my father-in-law entered and accidentally trod on me.

INNKEEPER *(explaining)*: On my son's behalf.

AZDAK *(to the* STABLEMAN*)*: You admit you started it?

STABLEMAN: Yes.

AZDAK: Ludovica, you like to eat sweet things?

LUDOVICA: Yes, sunflower seeds!

AZDAK: You like to lie a long time in the bathtub?

LUDOVICA: Half an hour or so.

AZDAK: Public Prosecutor, drop your knife—there on the ground. *(*SHAUWA *does so.)* Ludovica, pick up that knife. *(*LUDOVICA, *swaying her hips, does so.)* See that? *(He points* *at her.)* The way it moves? The rape is now proven. By eat-ing too much — sweet things, especially — by lying too long in warm water, by laziness and too soft a skin, you have raped that unfortunate man. Think you can run around with a behind like that and get away with it in court? This is a case of intentional assault with a dangerous weapon! You are sen-tenced to hand over to the Court the little roan which your father liked to ride "on his son's behalf." And now, come with me to the stables, so the Court can inspect the scene of the crime, Ludovica.

SINGER AND CHORUS:
When the sharks the sharks devour
Little fishes have their hour.
For a while the load is off their back.
On Grusinia's highways faring
Fixed-up scales of justice bearing
Strode the poor man's magistrate: Azdak.

And he gave to the forsaken
All that from the rich he'd taken.
And a bodyguard of roughnecks was Azdak's.
And our good and evil man, he
Smiled upon Grusinia's Granny.
His emblem was a tear in sealing wax.

All mankind should love each other
But when visiting your brother
Take an ax along and hold it fast.
Not in theory but in practice
Miracles are wrought with axes
And the age of miracles is not past.

AZDAK's *judge's chair is in a tavern. Three rich* FARMERS *stand before* AZDAK. SHAUWA *brings him wine. In a corner stands an* OLD PEASANT WOMAN. *In the open doorway, and outside, stand villagers looking on. An* IRONSHIRT *stands guard with a banner.*

AZDAK: The Public Prosecutor has the floor.

SHAUWA: It concerns a cow. For five weeks, the defendant has had a cow in her stable, the property of the farmer Suru. She was also found to be in possession of a stolen ham, and a number of cows belonging to Shutoff were killed after he asked the defendant to pay the rent on a piece of land.

FARMERS:

— It's a matter of my ham, Your Honor.

— It's a matter of my cow, Your Honor.

— It's a matter of my land, Your Honor.

AZDAK: Well, Granny, what have *you* got to say to all this?

OLD WOMAN: Your Honor, one night toward morning, five weeks ago, there was a knock at my door, and outside stood a bearded man with a cow. "My dear woman," he said, "I am the miracle-working Saint Banditus and because your son has been killed in the war, I bring you this cow as a souvenir. Take good care of it."

FARMERS:

— The robber, Irakli, Your Honor!

— Her brother-in-law, Your Honor!

— The cow-thief!

— The incendiary!

— He must be beheaded!

*Outside, a woman screams. The crowd grows restless, retreats. Enter the* BANDIT *Irakli with a huge ax.*

BANDIT: A very good evening, dear friends! A glass of vodka!

FARMERS (*crossing themselves*): Irakli!

AZDAK: Public Prosecutor, a glass of vodka for our guest. And who are you?

BANDIT: I'm a wandering hermit, Your Honor. Thanks for the gracious gift. (*He empties the glass which* SHAUWA *has brought.*) Another!

AZDAK: I am Azdak. (*He gets up and bows. The* BANDIT *also bows.*) The Court welcomes the foreign hermit. Go on with your story, Granny.

OLD WOMAN: Your Honor, that first night I didn't yet know Saint Banditus could work miracles, it was only the cow. But one night, a few days later, the farmer's servants came to take the cow away again. Then they turned round in front of my door and went off without the cow. And bumps as big as a fist sprouted on their heads. So I knew that Saint Banditus had changed their hearts and turned them into friendly people.

*The* BANDIT *roars with laughter.*

FIRST FARMER: I know what changed them.

AZDAK: That's fine. You can tell us later. Continue.

OLD WOMAN: Your Honor, the next one to become a good man was the farmer Shutoff—a devil, as everyone knows. But Saint Banditus arranged it so he let me off the rent on the little piece of land.

SECOND FARMER: Because my cows were killed in the field.

*The* BANDIT *laughs.*

OLD WOMAN (*answering* AZDAK'*s sign to continue*): Then one morning the ham came flying in at my window. It hit me in the small of the back. I'm still lame, Your Honor, look. (*She limps a few steps. The* BANDIT *laughs.*) Your Honor, was there ever a time when a poor old woman could get a ham *without* a miracle?

*The* BANDIT *starts sobbing.*

AZDAK (*rising from his chair*): Granny, that's a question that strikes straight at the Court's heart. Be so kind as to sit here. (*The* OLD WOMAN, *hesitating, sits in the judge's chair.*)

AZDAK (*sits on the floor, glass in hand, reciting*):
Granny
We could almost call you Granny Grusinia
The Woebegone
The Bereaved Mother
Whose sons have gone to war.
Receiving the present of a cow
She bursts out crying.

When she is beaten
She remains hopeful.
When she's not beaten
She's surprised.
On us
Who are already damned
May you render a merciful verdict
Granny Grusinia!
*(Bellowing at the* FARMERS:*)* Admit you don't believe in
miracles, you atheists! Each of you is sentenced to pay five
hundred piasters! For godlessness! Get out! *(The* FARMERS
*slink out.)* And you Granny, and you *(to the* BANDIT*)* pious
man, empty a pitcher of wine with the Public Prosecutor
and Azdak!

SINGER AND CHORUS:
And he broke the rules to save them.
Broken law like bread he gave them,
Brought them to shore upon his crooked back.
At long last the poor and lowly
Had someone who was not too holy
To be bribed by empty hands: Azdak.

For two years it was his pleasure
To give the beasts of prey short measure:
He became a wolf to fight the pack.
From All Hallows to All Hallows
On his chair beside the gallows
Dispensing justice in his fashion sat Azdak.

SINGER:
But the era of disorder came to an end.
The Grand Duke returned.
The Governor's wife returned.
A trial was held.
Many died.

The people's quarters burned anew.
And fear seized Azdak.

AZDAK *'s judge's chair stands again in the court of justice.* AZ-
DAK *sits on the floor, shaving and talking to* SHAUWA. *Noises
outside. In the rear the* FAT PRINCE *'s head is carried by on a
lance.*

AZDAK: Shauwa, the days of your slavery are numbered, maybe
even the minutes. For a long time now I have held you in
the iron curb of reason, and it has torn your mouth till it
bleeds. I have lashed you with reasonable arguments, I have
manhandled you with logic. You are by nature a weak man,
and if one slyly throws an argument in your path, you *have*
to snap it up, you can't resist. It is your nature to lick the
hand of some superior being. But superior beings can be of
very different kinds. And now, with your liberation, you will
soon be able to follow your natural inclinations, which are
low. You will be able to follow your infallible instinct, which
teaches you to plant your fat heel on the faces of men. Gone
is the era of confusion and disorder, which I find described
in the Song of Chaos. Let us now sing that song together in
memory of those terrible days. Sit down and don't do violence to the music. Don't be afraid. It sounds all right. And
it has a fine refrain. *(He sings.)*


THE SONG OF CHAOS IN EGYPT

Sister, hide your face! Brother, take your knife!
The times are out of joint!
Men of standing are wringing their hands,
Men of no standing are jumping for joy,
And this is what the city is saying:
"Let us drive the mighty from our midst!"
Offices are being raided, lists of serfs, destroyed.
Who lived always in darkness have come into the light

And have set master's nose to the grindstone
Have smashed the ebony poorbox to smithereens
Have sawn up the finest mahogany to make beds with.
Who had no bread at all have full granaries.
Who begged for corn on the corner now distribute it to others.

SHAUWA *(refrain)*. Oh, oh, oh, oh!
AZDAK *(refrain)*.

So where are you, General, where are you?
Restore order, restore order, please!

A nobleman's son can't be recognized now!
A lady's child can become her slave-girl's son!
The people's council is meeting in the barn.
At one time this fellow was lucky with a wall to sleep on:
Look, he's stretching his limbs on a bed!
At one time, this fellow rowed a boat, he owns ships now:
Their owner's looking for them, he's their owner no longer.
Those five men are being sent on a journey by their master:
"Go yourself," they say, "we have arrived."
*(The refrain is repeated.)*
Yes, so it might have been, had order been neglected much
longer. But now the Grand Duke has returned to the capi-
tal, and the Persians have lent him an army to restore order
with. The people's quarters are already aflame. Go and get
me the big book I always sit on. (SHAUWA *brings the big
book from the judge's chair.* AZDAK *opens it.)* This is the
Statute Book and I've always used it, as you can testify. Now
I'd better look in this book and see what they can do to me.
I've let the down-and-outs get away with murder, and I'll
have to pay for it. I helped poverty onto its skinny legs, so
they'll hang me for drunkenness. I peeped into the rich man's
pocket, which is bad taste. And I can't hide anywhere — everybody knows me because I've helped everybody.
SHAUWA: Someone's coming!

AZDAK *(in panic, he walks trembling to the chair)*: It's the end. And now they'd enjoy seeing what a Great Man I am. I'll deprive them of that pleasure. I'll beg on my knees for mercy. Spittle will slobber down my chin. The fear of death is in me.

*Enter Natella Abashwili, the* GOVERNOR'S WIFE, *followed by the* ADJUTANT *and an* IRONSHIRT.

GOVERNOR'S WIFE: What sort of a creature is that, Shalva?

AZDAK: A willing one, Your Highness, a man ready to oblige.

ADJUTANT: Natella Abashwili, wife of the late Governor, has just returned. She is looking for her two-year-old son, Michael. She has been informed that the child was carried off to the mountains by a former servant.

AZDAK: The child will be brought back, Your Highness, at your service.

ADJUTANT: They say that the person in question is passing it off as her own.

AZDAK: She will be beheaded, Your Highness, at your service.

ADJUTANT: That is all.

GOVERNOR'S WIFE *(leaving)*: I don't like that man.

AZDAK *(following her to door, bowing)*: At your service, Your Highness, it will all be arranged.

# 5

# The Chalk Circle

SINGER:

Hear now the story of the trial
Concerning Governor Abashwili's child
And the determination of the true mother
By the famous test of the Chalk Circle.
*Law court in Nuka.* IRONSHIRTS *lead* MICHAEL *across stage and out at the back.* IRONSHIRTS *hold* GRUSHA *back with their lances under the gateway until the child has been led through. Then she is admitted. She is accompanied by the former Governor's* COOK. *Distant noises and a fire-red sky.*

GRUSHA *(trying to hide)*: He's brave, he can wash himself now.

COOK: You're lucky. It's not a real judge. It's Azdak, a drunk who doesn't know what he's doing. The biggest thieves have got by through him. Because he gets everything mixed up and the rich never offer him big enough bribes, the likes of us sometimes do pretty well.

GRUSHA: I *need* luck right now.

COOK: Touch wood. *(She crosses herself.)* I'd better offer up another prayer that the judge may be drunk. *(She prays with motionless lips, while* GRUSHA *looks around, in vain, for the child.)* Why must you hold on to it at any price if it isn't yours? In days like these?

GRUSHA: He's mine. I brought him up.

COOK: Have you never thought what'd happen when she came back?

GRUSHA: At first I thought I'd give him to her. Then I thought she wouldn't come back.

COOK: And even a borrowed coat keeps a man warm, hm? *(*GRUSHA *nods.)* I'll swear to anything for you. You're a decent girl. *(She sees the soldier* SIMON SHASHAVA *approaching.)* You've done wrong by Simon, though. I've been talking with him. He just can't understand.

GRUSHA *(unaware of* SIMON*'s presence)*: Right now I can't be bothered whether he understands or not!

COOK: He knows the child isn't yours, but you married and not free "till death you do part" — he can't understand *that.*

GRUSHA *sees* SIMON *and greets him.*

SIMON *(gloomily)*: I wish the lady to know I will swear I am the father of the child.

GRUSHA *(low)*: Thank you, Simon.

SIMON: At the same time I wish the lady to know my hands are not tied — nor are hers.

COOK: You needn't have said that. You know she's married.

SIMON: And it needs no rubbing in.

*Enter an* IRONSHIRT.

IRONSHIRT: Where's the judge? Has anyone seen the judge?

ANOTHER IRONSHIRT *(stepping forward)*: The judge isn't here yet. Nothing but a bed and a pitcher in the whole house!

*Exeunt* IRONSHIRTS.

COOK: I hope nothing has happened to him. With any other judge you'd have as much chance as a chicken has teeth.

GRUSHA *(who has turned away and covered her face)*: Stand in front of me. I shouldn't have come to Nuka. If I run into the Ironshirt, the one I hit over the head . . .

*She screams. An* IRONSHIRT *had stopped and, turning his back, had been listening to her. He now wheels around. It is the* CORPORAL, *and he has a huge scar across his face.*

IRONSHIRT *(in the gateway)*: What's the matter, Shotta? Do you know her?

CORPORAL *(after staring for some time)*: No.

IRONSHIRT: She's the one who stole the Abashwili child, or so they say. If you know anything about it you can make some money, Shotta.

*Exit the* CORPORAL, *cursing.*

COOK: Was it him? *(*GRUSHA *nods.)* I think he'll keep his mouth shut, or he'd be admitting he was after the child.

GRUSHA: I'd almost forgotten him.

*Enter the* GOVERNOR'S WIFE, *followed by the* ADJUTANT *and two* LAWYERS.

GOVERNOR'S WIFE: At least there are no common people here, thank God. I can't stand their smell. It always gives me migraine.

FIRST LAWYER: Madam, I must ask you to be careful what you say until we have another judge.

GOVERNOR'S WIFE: But I didn't say anything, Illo Shuboladze. I love the people with their simple straightforward minds. It's only that their smell brings on my migraine.

SECOND LAWYER: There won't be many spectators. The whole population is sitting at home behind locked doors because of the riots in the people's quarters.

GOVERNOR'S WIFE *(looking at* GRUSHA*)*: Is that the creature?

FIRST LAWYER: Please, most gracious Natella Abashwili, abstain from invective until it is certain the Grand Duke has appointed a new judge and we're rid of the present one, who's about the lowest fellow ever seen in judge's gown. Things are all set to move, you see.

*Enter* IRONSHIRTS *from the courtyard.*

COOK: Her Grace would pull your hair out on the spot if she didn't know Azdak is for the poor. He goes by the face.

IRONSHIRTS *begin fastening a rope to a beam.* AZDAK, *in chains, is led in, followed by* SHAUWA, *also in chains. The three* FARMERS *bring up the rear.*

AN IRONSHIRT: Trying to run away, were you? *(He strikes* AZDAK.*)*

ONE FARMER: Off with his judge's gown before we string him up!

IRONSHIRTS *and* FARMERS *tear off Azdak's gown. His torn underwear is visible. Then someone kicks him.*

AN IRONSHIRT *(pushing him into someone else)*: Want a load of justice? Here it is!

*Accompanied by shouts of* "You take it!" *and* "Let me have him, Brother!" *they throw* AZDAK *back and forth until he collapses. Then he is lifted up and dragged under the noose.*

GOVERNOR'S WIFE *(who, during this "ballgame," has clapped her hands hysterically)*: I disliked that man from the moment I first saw him.

AZDAK *(covered with blood, panting)*: I can't see. Give me a rag.

AN IRONSHIRT: What is it you want to see?

AZDAK: You, you dogs! *(He wipes the blood out of his eyes with his shirt.)* Good morning, dogs! How goes it, dogs! How's the dog world? Does it smell good? Got another boot for me to lick? Are you back at each other's throats, dogs?

*Accompanied by a* CORPORAL, *a dust-covered* RIDER *enters. He takes some documents from a leather case, looks at them, then interrupts.*

RIDER: Stop! I bring a dispatch from the Grand Duke, containing the latest appointments.

CORPORAL *(bellowing)*: Atten-shun!

RIDER: Of the new judge it says: "We appoint a man whom we have to thank for saving a life indispensable to the country's welfare—a certain Azdak of Nuka." Which is he?

SHAUWA *(pointing)*: That's him, Your Excellency.

CORPORAL *(bellowing)*: What's going on here?

AN IRONSHIRT: I beg to report that His Honor Azdak was already His Honor Azdak, but on these farmers' denunciation was pronounced the Grand Duke's enemy.

CORPORAL *(pointing at the* FARMERS*)*: March them off! *(They are marched off. They bow all the time.)* See to it that His Honor Azdak is exposed to no more violence.

*Exeunt* RIDER *and* CORPORAL.

COOK *(to* SHAUWA*)*: She clapped her hands! I hope he saw it!

FIRST LAWYER: It's a catastrophe.

AZDAK *has fainted. Coming to, he is dressed again in judge's robes. He walks, swaying, toward the* IRONSHIRTS.

AN IRONSHIRT: What does Your Honor desire?

AZDAK: Nothing, fellow dogs, or just an occasional boot to lick. *(To* SHAUWA:*)* I pardon you. *(He is unchained.)* Get me some red wine, the sweet kind. *(*SHAUWA *stumbles off.)* Get out of here, I've got to judge a case. *(Exeunt* IRONSHIRTS. SHAUWA *returns with a pitcher of wine.* AZDAK *gulps it down.)* Something for my backside. *(*SHAUWA *brings the Statute Book, puts it on the judge's chair.* AZDAK *sits on it.)* I accept.

*The Prosecutors, among whom a worried council has been held, smile with relief. They whisper.*

COOK: Oh dear!

SIMON: A well can't be filled with dew, they say.

LAWYERS *(approaching* AZDAK, *who stands up, expectantly)*: A quite ridiculous case, Your Honor. The accused has abducted a child and refuses to hand it over.

AZDAK *(stretching out his hand, glancing at* GRUSHA*)*: A most attractive person. *(He fingers the money, then sits down, satisfied.)* I declare the proceedings open and demand the whole truth. *(To* GRUSHA:*)* Especially from you.

FIRST LAWYER: High Court of Justice! Blood, as the popular saying goes, is thicker than water. This old adage . . .

AZDAK *(interrupting)*: The Court wants to know the lawyers' fee.

FIRST LAWYER *(surprised)*: I beg your pardon? *(AZDAK, smiling, rubs his thumb and index finger.)* Oh, I see. Five hundred piasters, Your Honor, to answer the Court's somewhat unusual question.

AZDAK: Did you hear? The question is unusual. I ask it because I listen in quite a different way when I know you're good.

FIRST LAWYER *(bowing)*: Thank you, Your Honor. High Court of Justice, of all ties the ties of blood are strongest. Mother and child — is there a more intimate relationship? Can one tear a child from its mother? High Court of Justice, she has conceived it in the holy ecstasies of love. She has carried it in her womb. She has fed it with her blood. She has borne it with pain. High Court of Justice, it has been observed that the wild tigress, robbed of her young, roams restless through the mountains, shrunk to a shadow. Nature herself...

AZDAK *(interrupting, to GRUSHA)*: What's your answer to all this and anything else that lawyer might have to say?

GRUSHA: He's mine.

AZDAK: Is that all? I hope you can prove it. Why should I assign the child to you in any case?

GRUSHA: I brought him up like the priest says "according to my best knowledge and conscience." I always found him something to eat. Most of the time he had a roof over his head. And I went to such trouble for him. I had expenses too. I didn't look out for my own comfort. I brought the child up to be friendly with everyone, and from the beginning taught him to work. As well as he could, that is. He's still very little.

FIRST LAWYER: Your Honor, it is significant that the girl herself doesn't claim any tie of blood between her and the child.

AZDAK: The Court takes note of that.

FIRST LAWYER: Thank you, Your Honor. And now permit a woman bowed in sorrow — who has already lost her husband and now has also to fear the loss of her child — to

address a few words to you. The gracious Natella Abashwili
is...

GOVERNOR'S WIFE *(quietly)*: A most cruel fate, sir, forces me
to describe to you the tortures of a bereaved mother's soul,
the anxiety, the sleepless nights, the...

SECOND LAWYER *(bursting out)*: It's outrageous the way this
woman is being treated! Her husband's palace is closed to
her! The revenue of her estates is blocked, and she is cold-
bloodedly told that it's tied to the heir. She can't do a thing
without that child. She can't even pay her lawyers!! *(To the
FIRST LAWYER, who, desperate about this outburst, makes
frantic gestures to keep him from speaking:)* Dear Illo Shuboladze, surely it can be divulged now that the Abashwili estates are at stake?

FIRST LAWYER: Please, Honored Sandro Oboladze! We
agreed... *(To AZDAK:)* Of course it is correct that the trial
will also decide if our noble client can take over the Abashwili estates, which are rather extensive. I say "also" advised-
ly, for in the foreground stands the human tragedy of a
mother, as Natella Abashwili very properly explained in the
first words of her moving statement. Even if Michael Abashwili were not heir to the estates, he would still be the dearly
beloved child of my client.

AZDAK: Stop! The Court is touched by the mention of estates.
It's a proof of human feeling.

SECOND LAWYER: Thanks, Your Honor. Dear Illo Shuboladze,
we can prove in any case that the woman who took the
child is not the child's mother. Permit me to lay before the
Court the bare facts. High Court of Justice, by an unfortunate chain of circumstances, Michael Abashwili was left behind on that Easter Sunday while his mother was making
her escape. Grusha, a palace kitchen maid, was seen with
the baby...

COOK: All her mistress was thinking of was what dresses she'd
take along!

SECOND LAWYER *(unmoved)*: Nearly a year later Grusha turned up in a mountain village with a baby and there entered into the state of matrimony with . . .

AZDAK: How'd you get to that mountain village?

GRUSHA: On foot, Your Honor. And he was mine.

SIMON: I'm the father, Your Honor.

COOK: I used to look after it for them, Your Honor. For five piasters.

SECOND LAWYER: This man is engaged to Grusha, High Court of Justice: his testimony is suspect.

AZDAK: Are you the man she married in the mountain village?

SIMON: No, Your Honor, she married a peasant.

AZDAK *(to GRUSHA)*: Why? *(Pointing at SIMON.)* Is he no good in bed? Tell the truth.

GRUSHA: We didn't get that far. I married because of the baby. So he'd have a roof over his head. *(Pointing at SIMON.)* He was in the war, Your Honor.

AZDAK: And now he wants you back again, huh?

SIMON: I wish to state in evidence . . .

GRUSHA *(angrily)*: I am no longer free, Your Honor.

AZDAK: And the child, you claim, comes from whoring? *(GRUSHA doesn't answer.)* I'm going to ask you a question: What kind of child is he? A ragged little bastard? Or from a good family?

GRUSHA *(angrily)*: He's an ordinary child.

AZDAK: I mean — did he have refined features from the beginning?

GRUSHA: He had a nose on his face.

AZDAK: A very significant comment! It has been said of me that I went out one time and sniffed at a rosebush before rendering a verdict — tricks like that are needed nowadays. Well, I'll make it short, and not listen to any more lies. *(To GRUSHA:)* Especially not yours. *(To all the accused:)* I can imagine what you've cooked up to cheat me! I know you people. You're swindlers.

GRUSHA *(suddenly)*: I can understand your wanting to cut it short, now I've seen what you accepted!

AZDAK: Shut up! Did I accept anything from you?

GRUSHA *(while the* COOK *tries to restrain her)*: I haven't got anything.

AZDAK: Exactly. From starvelings I never get a thing. I might just as well starve, myself. You want justice, but do you want to pay for it, hm? When you go to a butcher you know you have to pay, but you people go to a judge as if you were off to a funeral supper.

SIMON *(loudly)*: When the horse was shod, the horsefly held out its leg, as the saying is.

AZDAK *(eagerly accepting the challenge)*: Better a treasure in manure than a stone in a mountain stream.

SIMON: A fine day. Let's go fishing, said the angler to the worm.

AZDAK: I'm my own master, said the servant, and cut off his foot.

SIMON: I love you as a father, said the Czar to the peasants, and had the Czarevitch's head chopped off.

AZDAK: A fool's worst enemy is himself.

SIMON: However, a fart has no nose.

AZDAK: Fined ten piasters for indecent language in court! That'll teach you what justice is.

GRUSHA *(furiously)*: A fine kind of justice! You play fast and loose with us because we don't talk as refined as that crowd with their lawyers.

AZDAK: That's true. You people are too dumb. It's only right you should get it in the neck.

GRUSHA: You want to hand the child over to her, and she wouldn't even know how to keep it dry, she's so "refined"! You know about as much about justice as I do!

AZDAK: There's something in that. I'm an ignorant man. Haven't even a decent pair of pants on under this gown. Look! With me, everything goes on food and drink — I was educated in a convent. Incidentally, I'll fine you ten piasters for

contempt of court. And you're a very silly girl, to turn me
against you, instead of making eyes at me and wiggling your
backside a little to keep me in a good temper. Twenty piasters!
GRUSHA: Even if it was thirty, I'd tell you what I think of your
justice, you drunken onion! *(Incoherently.)* How dare you talk
to me like the cracked Isaiah on the church window? As if
you were somebody? For you weren't born to this. You weren't
born to rap your own mother on the knuckles if she swipes
a little bowl of salt someplace. Aren't you ashamed of yourself when you see how I tremble before you? You've made
yourself their servant so no one will take their houses from
them — houses they had stolen! Since when have houses belonged to the bedbugs? But you're on the watch, or they
couldn't drag our men into their wars! You bribetaker!
AZDAK *half gets up, starts beaming. With his little hammer he
halfheartedly knocks on the table as if to get silence. As* GRUSHA'S
*scolding continues, he only beats time with his hammer.*
I've no respect for you. No more than for a thief or a bandit
with a knife! You can do what you want. You can take the
child away from me, a hundred against one, but I tell you
one thing: only extortioners should be chosen for a profession like yours, and men who rape children! As punishment!
Yes, let *them* sit in judgment on their fellow creatures. It is
worse than to hang from the gallows.
AZDAK *(sitting down)*: Now it'll be thirty! And I won't go on
squabbling with you — we're not in a tavern. What'd happen
to my dignity as a judge? Anyway, I've lost interest in your case.
Where's the couple who wanted a divorce? *(To* SHAUWA:*)*
Bring 'em in. This case is adjourned for fifteen minutes.
FIRST LAWYER *(to the* GOVERNOR'S WIFE*)*: Even without
using the rest of the evidence, Madam, we have the verdict
in the bag.
COOK *(to* GRUSHA*)*: You've gone and spoiled your chances
with him. You won't get the child now.
GOVERNOR'S WIFE: Shalva, my smelling salts!

*Enter a very old couple.*

AZDAK: I accept. *(The old couple don't understand.)* I hear you want to be divorced. How long have you been together?

OLD WOMAN: Forty years, Your Honor.

AZDAK: And why do you want a divorce?

OLD MAN: We don't like each other, Your Honor.

AZDAK: Since when?

OLD WOMAN: Oh, from the very beginning, Your Honor.

AZDAK: I'll think about your request and render my verdict when I'm through with the other case. (SHAUWA *leads them back.)* I need the child. *(He beckons* GRUSHA *to him and bends not unkindly toward her.)* I've noticed you have a soft spot for justice. I don't believe he's your child, but if he *were* yours, woman, wouldn't you want him to be rich? You'd only have to say he wasn't yours, and he'd have a palace and many horses in his stable and many beggars on his doorstep and many soldiers in his service and many petitioners in his court-yard, wouldn't he? What do you say—don't you want him to be rich?

GRUSHA *is silent.*

SINGER:

Hear now what the angry girl thought but did not say:
Had he golden shoes to wear
He'd be cruel as a bear
Evil would his life disgrace.
He'd laugh in my face.

Carrying a heart of flint
Is too troublesome a stint.
Being powerful and bad
Is hard on a lad.

Then let hunger be his foe!
Hungry men and women, no.
Let him fear the darksome night
But not daylight!

AZDAK: I think I understand you, woman.

GRUSHA *(suddenly and loudly)*: I won't give him up. I've raised him, and he knows me.

*Enter* SHAUWA *with the* CHILD.

GOVERNOR'S WIFE: He's in rags!

GRUSHA: That's not true. But I wasn't given time to put his good shirt on.

GOVERNOR'S WIFE: He must have been in a pigsty.

GRUSHA *(furiously)*: I'm not a pig, but there are some who are! Where did you leave your baby?

GOVERNOR'S WIFE: I'll show you, you vulgar creature! *(She is about to throw herself on* GRUSHA, *but is restrained by her lawyers.)* She's a criminal, she must be whipped. Immediately!

SECOND LAWYER *(holding his hand over her mouth)*: Natella Abashwili, you promised... Your Honor, the plaintiff's nerves...

AZDAK: Plaintiff and defendant! The Court has listened to your case, and has come to no decision as to who the real mother is; therefore, I, the judge, am obliged to *choose* a mother for the child. I'll make a test. Shauwa, get a piece of chalk and draw a circle on the floor. *(*SHAUWA *does so.)* Now place the child in the center. *(*SHAUWA *puts* MICHAEL, *who smiles at* GRUSHA, *in the center of the circle.)* Stand near the circle, both of you. *(The* GOVERNOR'S WIFE *and* GRUSHA *step up to the circle.)* Now each of you take the child by one hand. *(They do so.)* The true mother is she who can pull the child out of the circle.

SECOND LAWYER *(quickly)*: High Court of Justice, I object! The fate of the great Abashwili estates, which are tied to the child, as the heir, should not be made dependent on such a doubtful duel. In addition, my client does not command the strength of this person, who is accustomed to physical work.

AZDAK: She looks pretty well fed to me. Pull! *(The* GOVERNOR'S WIFE *pulls the* CHILD *out of the circle on her side;*

GRUSHA *has let go and stands aghast.)* What's the matter with you? You didn't pull.

GRUSHA: I didn't hold on to him.

FIRST LAWYER *(congratulating the* GOVERNOR'S WIFE*):* What did I say! The ties of blood!

GRUSHA *(running to* AZDAK*):* Your Honor, I take back everything I said against you. I ask your forgiveness. But could I keep him till he can speak all the words? He knows a few.

AZDAK: Don't influence the Court. I bet you only know about twenty words yourself. All right, I'll make the test once more, just to be certain. *(The two women take up their positions again.)* Pull! *(Again* GRUSHA *lets go of the* CHILD.*)*

GRUSHA *(in despair):* I brought him up! Shall I also tear him to bits? I can't!

AZDAK *(rising):* And in this manner the Court has determined the true mother. *(To* GRUSHA:*)* Take your child and be off. I advise you not to stay in the city with him. *(To the* GOVERNOR'S WIFE:*)* And you disappear before I fine you for fraud. Your estates fall to the city. They'll be converted into a playground for the children. They need one, and I've decided it'll be called after me: Azdak's Garden.

*The* GOVERNOR'S WIFE *has fainted and is carried out by the* LAWYERS *and the* ADJUTANT. GRUSHA *stands motionless.* SHAUWA *leads the* CHILD *toward her.*

Now I'll take off this judge's gown — it's got too hot for me. I'm not cut out for a hero. In token of farewell I invite you all to a little dance in the meadow outside. Oh, I'd almost forgotten something in my excitement . . . to sign the divorce decree. *(Using the judge's chair as a table, he writes something on a piece of paper, and prepares to leave. Dance music has started.)*

SHAUWA *(having read what is on the paper):* But that's not right. You've not divorced the old people. You've divorced Grusha!

AZDAK: Divorced the wrong couple? What a pity! And I never retract! If I did, how could we keep order in the land? *(To the old couple:)* I'll invite you to my party instead. You don't mind dancing with each other, do you? *(To* GRUSHA *and* SIMON:*)* I've got forty piasters coming from you.

SIMON *(pulling out his purse)*: Cheap at the price, Your Honor. And many thanks.

AZDAK *(pocketing the cash)*: I'll be needing this.

GRUSHA *(to* MICHAEL*)*: So we'd better leave the city tonight, Michael? *(To* SIMON:*)* You like him?

SIMON: With my respects, I like him.

GRUSHA: Now I can tell you: I took him because on that Easter Sunday I got engaged to you. So he's a child of love. Michael, let's dance.

*She dances with* MICHAEL, SIMON *dances with the* COOK, *the old couple with each other.* AZDAK *stands lost in thought. The dancers soon hide him from view. Occasionally he is seen, but less and less as more couples join the dance.*

SINGER:

And after that evening Azdak vanished and was never seen again.

The people of Grusinia did not forget him but long remembered

The period of his judging as a brief golden age,

Almost an age of justice.

*All the couples dance off.* AZDAK *has disappeared.*

But you, you who have listened to the Story of the Chalk Circle,

Take note what men of old concluded:

That what there is shall go to those who are good for it,

Children to the motherly, that they prosper,

Carts to good drivers, that they be driven well,

The valley to the waterers, that it yield fruit.

# Selected Bibliography

## PLAYS

*Baal*, 1918

*Trommeln in der Nacht* (Drums in the Night), 1918–20

*Im Dickicht der Städte* (In the Jungle of the Cities), 1921–23

*Mann ist Mann* (A Man's a Man), 1924–25

*Die Dreigroschenoper* (The Threepenny Opera), 1928

*Aufstieg und Fall der Stadt Mahagonny* (Rise and Fall of the City of Mahagonny), 1928–29

*Das Badener Lehrstück vom Einverständnis* (The Didactic Play of Baden: On Consent), 1928–29

*Die heilige Johanna der Schlachthöfe* (St. Joan of the Stockyards), 1929–30

*Die Massnahme* (The Measures Taken), 1930

*Die Mutter* (The Mother), 1930–32

*Die Rundköpfe und die Spitzköpfe* (Roundheads and Peakheads), 1931–36.

*Furcht und Elend des Dritten Reiches* (Fear and Misery in the Third Reich), 1935–38

*Mutter Courage und ihre Kinder* (Mother Courage and Her Children), 1939

*Das Verhör des Lukullus* (The Trial of Lucullus), 1939
*Leben des Galilei* (Galileo), 1938–40
*Der gute Mensch von Sezuan* (The Good Woman of Setzuan), 1938–40
*Herr Puntila und sein knecht Matti* (Mr. Puntila and His Man, Matti), 1940–41
*Der aufhaltsame Aufstieg des Arturo Ui* (The Resistible Rise of Arturo Ui), 1941
*Schweyk im zweiten Weltkrieg* (Schweik in the Second World War), 1941–44
*Die Gesichte der Simone Machard* (The Visions of Simone Machard), 1941–44
*Der kaukakische Kreidekreis* (The Caucasian Chalk Circle), 1944–45
*Antigone,* 1947
*Die Tage der Kommune* (Days of the Commune), 1948–49
*Der Hofmeister* (The Tutor), 1950
*Turandot,* 1953–54, unfinished

## TRANSLATED POEMS AND SONGS IN BOOK FORM

*Selected Poems.* Translated by H.R. Hays. New York: Reynal and Hitchcock, 1947.
*Manual of Piety.* Translated by Eric Bentley. New York: Grove Press, 1966.
*The Brecht-Eisler Song Book.* Edited, with translations by Eric Bentley. New York: Oak Publications, 1967 (later taken over by Music Sales Corporation, New York).
*Poems 1913–1956.* Edited by John Willett and Ralph Mannheim. London and New York: Methuen, 1976.

## THE BRECHT-BENTLEY RECORDINGS

*Bentley on Brecht: A Bertolt Brecht Miscellany.* Performed by Eric Bentley. Folkways, FH 5434.
*Brecht Before the Un-American Activities Committee.* A recording of the hearing. Folkways, FD 5531.

*The Elephant Calf.* The National Company cast album. Folkways, FL 9831.

*The Exception and the Rule.* The Off-Broadway cast album with Joseph Chaikin. Folkways, FL 9849.

*A Man's a Man.* The Off-Broadway cast album. Music by Joe Raposo. Spoken Arts, SA 870.

*Songs of Hanns Eisler.* Most of them to words by Brecht. Folkways, FH 5433.

The five Folkways recordings were originally twelve-inch LPs but today are distributed by Smithsonian Folkways as cassette tapes and CDs. The Spoken Arts album is available from P.O. Box 100, New Rochelle, NY 10802-0100.

## BIOGRAPHY AND CRITICISM

Bentley, Eric. *The Playwright as Thinker.* New York: Reynal and Hitchcock, 1946.

———. *The Brecht Commentaries.* New York: Grove Press; London: Eyre Methuen, 1981.

———. *The Brecht Memoir.* New York: PAJ Publications, 1985.

———. *Bertolt Brecht: A Study Guide.* New York: Grove, 1995.

———. *Bentley on Brecht.* New York: Applause, 1998.

Demetz, Peter, ed. *Brecht: A Collection of Critical Essays.* Englewood Cliffs, N.J.: Prentice-Hall, 1962.

Esslin, Martin. *Brecht: The Man and His Work.* Garden City, N.Y.: Doubleday Anchor, 1960.

Fuegi, John. *Bertolt Brecht: Chaos according to Plan.* Cambridge: Cambridge University Press, 1987.

———. *Brecht and Company.* New York: Grove, 1994.

Hayman, Ronald. *Brecht: a Biography.* New York: Oxford University Press, 1983.

Lyon, James K. *Bertolt Brecht in America.* Princeton: Princeton University Press, 1980.

Munk, Erika, ed. *Brecht.* New York: Bantam Books, 1972.

Spalter, Max. *Brecht's Tradition.* Baltimore, Md.: Johns Hopkins Press, 1967.

Volker, Klaus. *Brecht Chronicle.* Trans. Fred Wieck. New York: The Seabury Press, 1975.

———. *Brecht: A Biography.* Trans. John Nowell. New York: The Seabury Press, 1978.

Willett, John. *The Theatre of Bertolt Brecht.* Norfolk, Conn.: New Directions, 1959.

Witt, Hubert, ed. *Brecht as They Knew Him.* Trans. John Peet. New York: International Publishers, 1974.

**Bertolt Brecht** was born in Germany in 1898 and grew up amid the violence and turbulence of twentieth-century Europe. His experiences as a medical orderly in World War I and as a witness to the political and social turmoil in defeated Germany helped shape the Marxist vision that informed his poems and plays, beginning with *Baal* in 1918. One of the most influential writers in Germany in the years before 1933, with such triumphs to his credit as *The Threepenny Opera* and *Rise and Fall of the City of Mahagonny* (both with music by Kurt Weill), Brecht fled the country upon the Nazi assumption of power. *The Good Woman of Setzuan* was written in 1939–40, during a period of exile spent in Finland, and *The Caucasian Chalk Circle* was written in Hollywood in 1944. After World War II, Brecht returned to Europe, living first in Switzerland and then in East Germany, where he died in 1956.

**Eric Bentley,** one of the foremost authorities on the modern theater and a longtime intimate of Bertolt Brecht, has translated and edited most of Brecht's major works. He was born in Bolton, Lancashire, in 1916 and became an American citizen in 1948. He began his professional career as a scholar, went on to become a drama critic and translator, and then became a playwright. He was inducted into the Theatre Hall of Fame in 1998.